"A really outstanding guide, not jus
but to being a Christian disciple in
profound human intelligence, insig.

—Rowan Williams

"This discussion of the Rule of Saint Benedict is more than the stringing together of a series of pious paraphrases that are already familiar to the reader. It engages with the Rule by serious excavation of its scriptural foundations and also by setting it in conversation with the issues and difficulties of the contemporary world, both within the church and within postmodern society. The resulting conclusions are profound and stimulating, and accessible to the ordinary reader."

—Michael Casey, OCSO

"Luigi Gioia's meditations on the Rule of St. Benedict not only encapsulate and distill his long experience of the monastic life, but offer this wisdom, with striking theological profundity, to a wider reading public. Steeped in Scripture and tradition, but no less animated by modern psychological insight, this little book is an unusual spiritual gem that will stand the test of time."

—Sarah Coakley
Norris-Hulse Professor of Divinity Emerita
University of Cambridge

"In *Saint Benedict's Wisdom* Luigi Gioia constructively lays out a Benedictine spirituality for the twenty-first century. Weaving together a rich tapestry of insights and experiences from his years as a monk and scholar, Gioia demonstrates anew that the wisdom of the Rule of Benedict remains relevant, not only for the monk, but for the church and even for the world. He shows that the Rule's catholicity gives it a vantage point from which it offers guidance to all of humanity in how to live and love well. Gioia not only confirms the Rule of Benedict's place among the Christian tradition's sapiential literature, but *Saint Benedict's Wisdom* itself is a product of wisdom, from the hand of one sufficiently wise to offer it."

—Rev. Greg Peters, PhD, SMD

"An inviting, accessible, and above all wise investigation into what the Rule of St. Benedict, that treasure house of Christian spirituality, can teach us about wisdom. This subtle book is meant not simply for the monk or even the Benedictine aficionado but all Christians seeking the path to Wisdom, which is to say to God."

—James Martin, SJ, author of *Jesus: A Pilgrimage*

"Gioia's forthright overview of monastic spirituality and its contemporary issues challenges all monastics to be a prophetic voice in the church and the world."

—Judith Sutera, OSB, Mount St. Scholastica, Kansas

"At a time when all our forms of institutional belonging are being shaken up, my friend Luigi Gioia does a wonderful job at showing how St. Benedict's wisdom is both centered and flexible, making it available for us as we feel out the new wine skins into which the Gospel is pouring us."

—James Alison, Catholic theologian, priest, and author of *Knowing Jesus*

Saint Benedict's Wisdom

Monastic Spirituality and the Life of the Church

Luigi Gioia, OSB

translated by Barry Hudock

LITURGICAL PRESS
Collegeville, Minnesota

www.litpress.org

Cover design by Ann Blattner. Photo by Greg Becker.

Originally published as *La saggezza del monaco* by Luigi Gioia © 2017 C.E.D. Centro Editoriale Dehoniano Srl, Bologna, Italy.

1   2   3   4   5   6   7   8   9

Library of Congress Cataloging-in-Publication Data

Names: Gioia, Luigi, 1968– author. | Hudock, Barry, translator.
Title: Saint Benedict's wisdom : monastic spirituality and the life of the church / Luigi Gioia ; translated by Barry Hudock.
Other titles: Saggezza del monaco. English
Description: Collegeville, Minnesota : Liturgical Press, [2020] | "Originally published as La saggezza del monaco by Luigi Gioia © 2017 C.E.D. Centro Editoriale Dehoniano Srl, Bologna, Ital"—Colophon. | Summary: "Luigi Gioia, OSB, demonstrates the many ways that monastic spirituality is a gift for the whole Church and every baptized Christian"— Provided by publisher.
Identifiers: LCCN 2020002935 (print) | LCCN 2020002936 (ebook) | ISBN 9780814688083 (paperback) | ISBN 9780814688335 (epub) | ISBN 9780814688335 (mobi) | ISBN 9780814688335 (pdf)
Subjects: LCSH: Monastic and religious life. | Benedictines—Spiritual life. | Benedict, Saint, Abbot of Monte Cassino. Regula. | Spiritual life—Catholic Church.
Classification: LCC BX2435 .G44613 2020 (print) | LCC BX2435 (ebook) | DDC 248.8/94—dc23
LC record available at https://lccn.loc.gov/2020002935
LC ebook record available at https://lccn.loc.gov/2020002936

To Rowan,
who taught me the value of patience
in the hard work of sustaining difference
as the form of ecclesial love.

Contents

Introduction

What is being "made" in the workshop [of Benedictine monasticism] is souls—bodily human beings who understand themselves with growing clarity and are engaged in creating a durable life together.

Rowan Williams[1]

I remember well how, at age 18, I spent the first months of my novitiate in a Benedictine monastery deeply resenting the piercing corridor bell that woke me up before dawn every morning for Matins. Struggling to emerge from my uneasy sleep, I would invariably wonder what on earth I was doing in that place.

It was just an initial reaction, and as soon as I had washed my face with cold water and recovered my wits, my resentment was replaced by a feeling of genuine excitement about the day that lay ahead. Then one day I came across a sentence from the Bible that changed everything: "Whoever gets up early to seek her [Wisdom] will have no trouble but will find her sitting at the door" (Wis 6:14, my translation).[2] I remember being immediately seduced by the idea that waking up early every morning was more than just obeying a rule or fulfilling a duty. It appeared to me as a step in a quest for wisdom, with the promise that my perception of things

---

1. Rowan Williams, "Follow St Benedict's Rule," *The Oldie*, December 30, 2019: https://www.theoldie.co.uk/blog/follow-st-benedicts-rule.

2. All Scripture quotations are from the New American Bible, Revised Edition, unless otherwise noted.

would change over time and I would start experiencing them in a deeper and more meaningful way—and especially that I would start enjoying those very things that I still found upsetting or irritating.

What endeared Wisdom to me was this image of her sitting at my door, ready to walk with me and to teach me how to find delight in God's presence and in the company of people. We are told that she is "daily [God's] delight, rejoicing before him always" and also that she "rejoic[es] in his inhabited world and delight[s] in the human race" (Prov 8:30-31, NRSV). Delighting and rejoicing: is this not what we are all looking for?

This book stems from that initial realization and is rooted in the following decades of life in several communities in Italy and France and of preaching retreats in monasteries all over the world, including China, Korea, Australia, Philippines, Canada, and the US. Wisdom is not just a quality we acquire, but something—or better, *someone*—we are called to become. This, I think, is the reason she is personified in Scripture. We become her by learning from her to find delight in the company of God and of our sisters and brothers and by opening our inner ears to the anointing within (cf. 1 John 2:20).

In the history of Christianity—or better, of the whole of humanity—Wisdom takes a bewildering variety of forms. This book explores the Wisdom that has developed in Christian monasticism owing to one of her greatest friends, the sixth century monk Benedict of Nursia (480–547), who describes the monastery as the *school* were monastics learn how to serve God, the *workshop* where they handle the tools of good works, and the *house* governed *a sapientibus et sapienter*, that is, by monastics who have become friends of Wisdom (cf. Rule of Benedict [RB] 53.22).

Even though the work that Benedict handed down to future generations is called "The Rule," and indeed contains a number of instructions and norms, it would be a mistake to approach it as a legislative text.[3] None of today's countless communities of

---

3. In his recent, delightful book on Benedictine spirituality, Rowan Williams observes that historically the Rule has been understood as "a supremely useful

monks and nuns known as "Benedictine" treats the Rule in this way—in fact, their daily life is regulated by specific collections of regulations variously known as customaries, constitutions, or directories. Benedict's Rule endures rather as a source of inspiration. Monastics tirelessly read, meditate, and comment on it to unearth its many gems of prudence and discretion. It should be seen as an instance of the literary genre known as "sapiential" (from *sapientia*, "wisdom") or, better, of the sapiential vein that runs through the whole of Scripture.

We, too, therefore, shall expound the Rule's spiritual insights in the light of the biblical books of Proverbs and Wisdom. People who read the Rule for the first time can find it dry, be put off by some of its prescriptive portions, and entirely overlook its spiritual value and its significance for the life of the church and of society today. A monk once told me that only with old age had he become able to grasp the real depth and breadth of Benedict's wisdom.

Two principles have guided my own modest attempt to learn from this wisdom.

First, the conviction that the Rule is not meant to be read in isolation. It is not a self-referential text—if anything, it is totally "other-referential." Its final chapter makes this clear by inviting monastics not to confine themselves to the reading of the Rule but to complement it with a variety of other Christian texts, not only from monastic literature, but by any of the *catholici patres*, that is, theologians, biblical commentators, or spiritual authors.

Second, and more important, it has become increasingly clear to me that the best way to disclose Benedict's treasures of wisdom is to read his Rule in the light of Scripture, or rather, of the Word of God (this distinction is essential, as we shall see). Benedict's mind, prayer, imagination, and memory were entirely molded by his continuous meditation upon Scripture. Famously, the Rule was described as the quintessence of the Gospel by the

---

digest of monastic *theology*" rather than "a self-sufficient 'code'" (*The Way of St Benedict* [London: Bloomsbury, 2020], 91).

seventeenth-century French bishop Jacques-Bénigne Bossuet,[4] and indeed it is a tapestry of Scriptural quotations and allusions. However, the Rule's exceptional fruitfulness in this respect does not simply consist in the fact that it quotes the Bible but in its proven ability to teach us how to listen to the living word of God *through* the letter of Scripture.

This last point is the key to Benedictine spirituality and one of the main arguments of this book (especially in chapters 9, 10, and 11)—it is not an accident that the first word of the Rule is *Ausculta*, "Listen." And its ambition of teaching monastics how to listen to the many ways God speaks to us can be detected especially in its emphasis on life, movement, keenness, zeal. Thus we shall see that Benedict sees monastic life as *action* (chapter 9) or as the conversion from a vicious to a *virtuous circle* (chapter 11), or again how the only way to establish whether people truly are called to embrace monastic life is whether they are willing to remain *entirely in motion* (chapter 3). This principle shapes formation (chapter 3), leadership (chapter 4), forgiveness (chapter 5), chastity (chapter 6), and prayer (chapter 7).

This decisive connection to the living word of God by which monastic life stands or falls lies behind the cornerstone of Benedictine spirituality—namely, the principle that "nothing is to be preferred to the Work of God."[5] We will discover that this sentence doesn't simply mean that "nothing is more important than the celebration of the liturgy." If Benedict speaks of *"opus Dei"* ("work of God") rather than *"opus hominis"* ("work of people"), it is because he is not describing something that *we* do, but something that *God* does! *"Nihil operi Dei praeponatur"* means that nothing is more important than welcoming the work through which *the Lord* constantly speaks to us (chapter 2, 11, and especially the Conclusion).

---

4. Jacques-Bénigne Bossuet, *Oeuvres de Bossuet: Sermons. Panégyriques. Méditations sur l'évangile* (Paris: Firmin Didot Frères, 1866), 435.

5. *Rule of Saint Benedict 1980*, ed. Timothy Fry (Collegeville, MN: Liturgical Press, 1981) (hereafter, RB), 43.3.

It is, of course, always anachronistic to talk about "spirituality" in the case of any early Christian author like Benedict. Throughout the first millennium, Christians took for granted the identity between faith understood as loving and heartfelt trust in God (which we now call "spirituality") and faith as beliefs, doctrines, and creeds (which we call "theology"). Today, we live in the aftermath of the divorce between theology and spirituality,[6] and for our mindset there is no way of talking about prayer, interiority, experience of God, or self-knowledge without constantly having to make clear how they are related to God's identity as Father, Son, and Holy Spirit, to Jesus' reconciliation, to the church, and to Scripture (chapters 8 and 9).

Probably no epithet captures Benedictine spirituality more aptly than *healthy*, in the sense of "respecting and promoting the human flourishing of the whole person." Many modern readers are nonplussed, for example, by the extent to which a spiritual text like the Rule is far more concerned with the body than with the "soul" or the "inner life"—that is, with the supposed "place" in us where we would have access to some form of immediate experience of God.

In fact, Benedict spends most of his time talking about eating, sleeping, working, reading, talking, smiling—even "nature's needs" (RB 8.4) (that is, going to the bathroom!)—and especially about toiling in community life. He has no illusions about the inevitable hardships of life in common, otherwise he would not have poured out so much ink offering guidance meant to prevent character assassination (cf. his many passages on gossiping and grumbling) or to make clear that monastics should resist the occasional urge to kill or punch each other (RB 4.3, 4.70, and 70).

And yet all these factors are deeply "spiritual" in Benedict's mind. For him, the heathiest way of seeking God is through community

---

6. I borrow this expression from François Vandenbroucke in his article "Le divorce entre théologie et mystique: Ses origines," *Nouvelle Revue Théologique* 82 (1950): 372–387.

life, because he knows instinctively what phenomenology is redis-covering in our day—namely, that there is no access to interiority other than through interaction with our environment and others and no relation with God other than through the mediations of body, fellowship, history, and Scripture (chapter 8).

In so doing, the Rule echoes biblical and patristic writings on the nature of the fellowship that gathers all the baptized—that is, the church. This teaching was reclaimed by the Second Vatican Council, especially in the documents on the nature of the church (*Lumen Gentium*) and the relationship of the church with the world (*Gaudium et Spes*). The spiritual potential of these two docu-ments remains largely untapped. The tumultuous reception of the council and the ideological battles about its application that are still raging often rely on superficial or secondhand readings of these documents. In fact, just like the Rule, *Lumen Gentium* and *Gaudium et Spes*, too, should be read as sapiential texts—that is, as invitations not to be afraid of secularity or of taking processes and history seriously. Secularity, diversity, conflicts, and flaws are not to be feared but welcomed with a spirit of dialogue and especially with the greatest of ecclesial virtues, *patience*. Patience is para-mount because God saves us through time, waits for us as long as it takes, walks with us, remains with us until the end of time with his reconciling, comforting, enlightening presence (chapter 12).

It is true that Benedictine monasticism advocates a measure of detachment from secular lifestyle. The purpose of this distance, however, is not to evade history or repudiate secularity but to cultivate a deeper solidarity with the world and a greater com-passion for the sufferings of humanity. This distance is the space necessary to listen more attentively to the signs of times. Monastic life reminds the church of the priority of the desert in Christian action (chapter 2) and of the church's vocation to be the sign of a humanity which, despite its shortcomings, tries to remain open to the unendingly patient reconciling action of its Lord (Conclusion).

Finally, no honest portrayal of Benedictine monasticism can evade grappling with some aspects of its present crisis, especially in the West, and its need for recovering the potential for renewal inscribed in its DNA (chapter 11). The renewal of monasticism is crucial for the life of the whole church. The most eloquent proclamation of the Gospel is a fellowship that does not need to be perfect (and never will be on this side of the eschaton), but that should nonetheless be able to give witness to the healing power of the good news of God's love for humanity. This is what Jesus himself proclaims when he states, "This is how all will know that you are my disciples, if you have love for one another" (John 13:35). The real mission of Benedictine monasticism is to preserve the priority of community life, not out of self-interest but because love—that is, lived fellowship—alone is credible (see especially the Conclusion).

CHAPTER I

The Monastic Vocation: Wisdom or Folly?

> *[Benedict is] reminding us that it's very problematic to try to be too spiritual too soon.*
>
> Rowan Williams[1]

A promise not always kept

"Let whoever is inexperienced turn in here" (Prov 9:4, 16, my translation). In the book of Proverbs, we find this invitation on the lips of both Wisdom and Folly.[2] Their invitations are similar,

1. Williams, *The Way of St Benedict*, 41.
2. It is helpful to see the invitation in the context of the full passage:
   "Wisdom has built her house,
       she has set up her seven columns;
   She has prepared her meat, mixed her wine,
       yes, she has spread her table.
   She has sent out her maidservants; she calls
       from the heights out over the city:
   'Let whoever is naive [inexperienced] turn in here;
       to any who lack sense I say,
   Come, eat of my food,
       and drink of the wine I have mixed!
   Forsake foolishness that you may live;
       advance in the way of understanding.'

presented in the same words, though the outcomes are diametrically opposed—life in one case, death in the other. So the key questions are how to distinguish wisdom and folly from each other and how free we actually are in making our choice.

The choices that determine our lives are inevitably conditioned. Absolute freedom, unbound by any constraint, remains a prerogative of God alone. We do not get to view our lives from an elevated tower, from which we can serenely contemplate all possible options and then make the best choices with utter detachment, complete neutrality, and total objectivity. Contingency plays a role in most of our life choices.

This observation is not incompatible with belief in YHWH. Certainly such faith makes us aware of a God who "probe[s] me" and "know[s] me," who has "knit me in my mother's womb," and in whose book all our days are written (Ps 139:1, 13, 16). This God has a plan of salvation and desires life for each of us. This is a God who calls us. But this is also a God who takes history utterly seriously, through and through, a God who lets us take full responsibility as protagonists of our own lives and who therefore accepts that we will sometimes become tripped up by our own mistakes or negligence. This is a God who is great enough to be able to integrate completely—never pretending—our historicity, our fallibility, and even our sin.

. . .

Woman Folly is raucous,
    utterly foolish; she knows nothing.
She sits at the door of her house
    upon a seat on the city heights,
Calling to passersby
    as they go on their way straight ahead:
'Let those who are naive [inexperienced] turn in here,
    to those who lack sense I say,
Stolen water is sweet,
    and bread taken secretly is pleasing!'
Little do they know that the shades are there,
    that her guests are in the depths of Sheol!" (Prov 9:1-6, 13-18)

If the call of wisdom were easily distinguishable from that of folly, there would be no problem. But the disquieting warning of the book of Proverbs is that sometimes the calls of wisdom and of folly resemble each other, to the point of being offered with identical words: "Let whoever is inexperienced turn in here." Leaving aside dishonest appeals from those who might try deliberately to deceive us, let us limit ourselves to considering for a moment those who claim to call in the name of wisdom. We can begin by observing that just because the one issuing the invitation says it's offered in the name of God, that doesn't mean it guarantees access to wisdom. Visitors to Harlem in New York City pass by buildings of many Christian churches with colorful names—First Corinthian Church, Canaan Church, New Mount Zion Baptist Church—one after another, each competing with the other. Each of them claims to offer the most authentic version of the Gospel message; each is sure it offers the genuine invitation: "Let whoever is inexperienced come here!" How can one discern which of them calls in the name of wisdom and which in the name of folly?

The boundary between wisdom and folly can become even thinner in the case of the monastic vocation. Monastic life is a response to a call. A monastery's setting on a mountain or in a valley, its beauty, and the lifestyle that is led there all exert a charm, an attraction, a summons, and a call. A monastery grows only if new people continue to become part of it. Furthermore, it is not enough for a person to respond to this appeal once and for all. The dynamism of monastic life depends on a daily call that requires a continual response. It is a call to which one must incline one's ear (as the prologue of the Rule of Benedict puts it) uninterruptedly: "Listen carefully, my son, to the master's instructions, and attend to them with the ear of your heart. This is advice from a father who loves you; welcome it, and faithfully put it into practice. The labor of obedience will bring you back to him from whom you had drifted through the sloth of disobedience" (RB Prol. 1-2).

One enters a monastery to search for God—*Deum quaerere*—to seek life, and to make one's days happy: "Seeking his workman in a multitude of people, the Lord calls out to him and lifts his voice again: 'Is there anyone here who yearns for life and desires to see good days?' If you hear this and your answer is 'I do,' God then directs these words to you" (RB Prol. 14-16). This is the promise made to a young person who knocks on the doors of a monastery. The monastic life is offered as the way of wisdom mentioned in Proverbs 9:1-6.

The truth, unfortunately, is often different. Many monasteries claim to offer wisdom but then fail to keep this promise. Anyone who knows monastic realities up close has witnessed this tragedy. How many young people enter a monastery to look for God and instead find pettiness, misery, worldliness? How many who are thirsting for meaning, guidance, and experience find themselves at the mercy of formators or guides who are incompetent, disillusioned, and sometimes even dissolute? How many seek wisdom but are unfortunately unaware of (as Proverbs 9:18 puts it) the dark aspects of the monasteries they enter? The boundary between wisdom and folly is often unclear, and the switch from one to the other can happen almost unnoticed.

So what is the meaning of such a scandal? How to reconcile such a paradox? We will proceed in stages and begin with a description of an ideal situation in which wisdom would be all on one side and folly on the other.

The school built by Wisdom

Benedictine monasticism is different from the many forms of religious life established in the early Middle Ages, which are more or less centralized and characterized by great mobility and specialization. Benedict of Nursia did not establish an order: rather, he gathered a set of principles about living an evangelical and ascetic life, the fruit of his decades of experience, into a short summary that has passed through the centuries as the Rule of Benedict. All those communities that have drawn inspiration from this Rule in various forms of life, often without any institutional link between them, have been known as "Benedictine."

Pope Gregory the Great (540–604), in his *Dialogues*, presents Benedict as the heir of Jacob, Joseph, Elijah, and Elisha—friends of God formed by Wisdom who "passing into holy souls from age to age . . . produces friends of God and prophets" (Wis 7:27). A friend of Wisdom, Benedict set up "seven columns" (cf. Prov 9:1), not in a stone building, but by shaping the hearts of monastics according to the seven gifts of the Spirit: wisdom, understanding, counsel, fortitude, knowledge, piety, and fear of the Lord (cf. Isa 11:2, Vulgate). He also literally "prepare[d] a table," baking bread, pressing wine, cutting beef. Benedictine wisdom, summarized as *"ora et labora"* ("prayer and work"), manifests itself not only in the ordering of common prayer but also in that of food, sleep, manual work, and clothing. These aspects occupy most of the Rule. Everything in a monastery must speak of God—architecture, the garden, the good taste of food and wine, professionalism in work. All these aspects of life are an integral part of the pedagogy through which the monk "forsake[s] foolishness," "lives," and follows "the way of understanding" (Prov 9:6).

The Benedictine monastery is therefore one of the many houses built by Wisdom throughout history for the "inexperienced" and the ignorant, according to the pattern of YHWH's characteristic way of acting: pitching a tent in the midst of a people in order to gather them in a place of refreshment, without taking them out of the world, without interrupting their pilgrimage, but offering them rest and inspiration thanks to which they can take the road again with renewed enthusiasm. The Gospel of John says that in Christ, God "made his dwelling [literally, pitched his tent] among us" (John 1:14).

More particularly, the form assumed by this tent, by the house built by Wisdom through Benedict's ministry, is the *dominici schola servitii*, the "school for the Lord's service" announced at the end of his Rule's prologue: "Therefore we intend to establish a school for the Lord's service. In drawing up its regulations, we hope to set down nothing harsh, nothing burdensome" (RB Prol. 45-46).

The use of the word *service* to indicate what is learned in this school is rich in meaning from the biblical point of view. The liturgical worship of God is sometimes called "serving" God in the Scripture (for example, 2 Sam 15:8), and the Rule in fact prescribes that "nothing is to be preferred to the Work of God"—that is, to the community's liturgical prayer (RB 43.3). But more profoundly, God's servant is the one whom the Lord calls to collaborate in his plan of salvation. It is a title given to Moses (Exod 14:31), David (2 Sam 7:8), the patriarchs, the prophets, the priests, and finally to the Servant par excellence of Isaiah 49–55, whose ear is opened by the Lord to make him a privileged instrument in his work of salvation (Isa 50:4-5).

The parable of monastic life embodies the whole history of salvation: in Adam we have disobeyed, and in the obedience of Christ we find the way back to the Father. "Attend to [the master's instructions] with the ear of your heart. . . . The labor of obedience will bring you back to him from whom you had drifted through the sloth of disobedience" (RB Prol. 1-2).

The response to God's call is personal, but the call embraces the whole history of humanity.

That Benedict would establish a *school* of this service is good news, because it means that performing such service is not spontaneous or innate, but something that has to be learned. This is why we need a school—we need time, and above all we need a teacher. It is not the best and the perfect who are called to this school, but the inexperienced and the ignorant, those who need to learn.

The pedagogy of this school is that of Proverbs 9:1-6. Wisdom prepares the table, and she invites us to eat the bread and drink the wine that she has prepared. To those who are inexperienced and ignorant, she says, "Taste and see that the LORD is good" (Ps 34:9). In fact, the first thing that one is invited to discover at the home of Wisdom—that is, in the school for the Lord's service— is precisely this: the *taste for the things of God.* Then there is another moment in this transition from inexperience and ignorance to wisdom: access to understanding—that is, to a new perception of oneself and the world that comes through the widening of the heart that happens when one is nourished at the table of wisdom. This self-knowledge is a keystone of Benedictine asceticism—not just any self-knowledge, but that which unfolds in the light of God's mercy. We can, then, summarize the strategy of wisdom as Benedict took it up: (1) to establish a *school* for the Lord's service that (2) awakens one's *taste for the things of God*, helps one experience the goodness of God, and in this way (3) opens up a more authentic *understanding* of oneself, others, and the world. Having explored the first aspect of this strategy so far, let's consider the other two.

A taste for the things of God

It is no coincidence that the passage of Proverbs 9 mentioned above uses the metaphor of food to depict wisdom, because the Latin word for wisdom, *sapere*, includes the sense of "tasting" in its meaning. We read:

> [Wisdom] has prepared her meat, mixed her wine,
>   yes, she has spread her table. . . .
> [She calls out,] "Come, eat of my food,
>   and drink of the wine I have mixed!" (Prov 9:2, 5)

Most people who have visited or lived in a foreign country have experienced how at first the local foods might not seem very tasty, and sometimes they may even provoke disgust. Only slowly do visitors discover local flavors, their palate adapts to these flavors, and they begin to enjoy these foods and eat them happily. The monastic tradition refers to a similar process by talking of the awakening of one's "spiritual senses."

Each of us possesses a spiritual sense of hearing, taste, smell, vision, and touch. In the beginning, these senses are dull and unable to perceive the things of God. When this is the case, participation in community prayer is riddled with distractions, the word of God bores us and says nothing to us, silence is unbearable, and the life of the community seems like a waste of time. But progressively these inner senses become more refined, and monastics begin to find both nourishment and delight from the new foods of God's word, praise, silence, and common life, embracing them not because the Rule prescribes them, but willingly. Wisdom teaches monastics to appreciate the taste of common prayer, to allow themselves to be captured by the word of God, to love silence and inhabit it. Benedict's Rule describes this process as a gradual widening of the heart: "We hope to set down nothing harsh, nothing burdensome. The good of all concerned, however, may prompt us to a little strictness in order to amend faults and to safeguard love. Do not be daunted immediately by fear. . . . As we progress in this way of life and in faith, we shall run on the path of God's commandments, our hearts overflowing with the inexpressible delight of love" (RB Prol. 46-49).

So the monastic shouldn't be troubled if, as this taste develops, he or she goes through phases of disgust, boredom, sadness, or discouragement—they are inevitable along the journey of growth. To continue the metaphor used earlier, in a foreign country loneliness and disorientation can be overwhelming at first, and it takes time to adapt. The temptation may be to flee, to try to escape the boredom and disgust, but one must bravely face them and will eventually find oneself on the other side.

In this process, the patience and perseverance (*hypomoné* in the New Testament) to which the Rule of Benedict calls monastics are of great help: "Never swerving from his instructions, then, but faithfully observing his teaching in the monastery until death, we shall through patience share in the sufferings of Christ that we may deserve also to share in his kingdom" (RB Prol.50). The monastic "embraces suffering and endures it without weakening or seeking escape. For Scripture says, 'Anyone who perseveres to the end will be saved'" (RB 7.36, citing Matt 10:22).

A crucial part of this patient and persevering process of awakening one's spiritual senses, developing one's taste for the things of

God, and expanding one's heart is the role played by the spiritual guide. The spiritual guide is an experienced sister or a brother who helps the younger monastics constantly to reflect on the meaning of their experience and who can comfort them with God's own comfort (cf. 2 Cor 1:4).

Left alone, without the benefit of such an experienced spiritual father or mother, the monastic, rather than gaining wisdom and developing a taste for the things of God, can be overtaken by disgust and discouragement and sink slowly into despair. Thus, almost without realizing it, the boundary between wisdom and foolishness is crossed, and the monastic seeks relief in "stolen water" and "bread taken secretly" (Prov 9:17), a well-known phenomenon in the field of monastic spirituality traditionally called *acedia*.

Evagrius teaches us that acedia is essentially an escape from oneself and from the call of God.[3] Acedia is not a simple sadness, negligence of prayer, laziness, or lukewarmness. It is a loss of the taste for the food offered by wisdom (*tristitia de bono divino*), with the consequence that we no longer find joy in doing good or in walking the path of life (*tedium operandi*).[4] One can move from acedia to discouragement, then to despair, and finally to depression. And then what was supposed to be a school for the Lord's service, the house of wisdom, turns out to be a trap and "her guests are in the depths of Sheol!" (Prov 9:18).

Self-knowledge

Wisdom's assurance is that thanks to her we will "advance in the way of understanding" (Prov 9:6). In the school for the Lord's service, Benedict portrays this way as a *ladder*:

---

3. Cf. Evagrius Ponticus, *The Praktikos & Chapters on Prayer*, trans. John Eudes Bamberger (Kalamazoo, MI: Cistercian, 1981), 18–19.

4. Cf. Jean-Charles Nault, *La Saveur de Dieu: L'acédie dans le dynamisme de l'âme* (Paris: Cerf, 2006).

Brethren, divine Scripture calls to us saying: *Whoever exalts himself shall be humbled, and whoever humbles himself shall be exalted* (Luke 14:11; 18:14). . . . . Accordingly . . . by our ascending actions we must set up that ladder on which Jacob in a dream saw *angels ascending and descending* (Gen 28:12). Without doubt, this ascent and descent can signify only that we descend by exaltation and ascend by humility. Now the ladder erected is our life on earth, and if we humble our hearts the Lord will raise it to heaven. We may call our body and soul the sides of this ladder, into which our divine vocation has fitted the various steps of humility and discipline as we ascend. (RB 7.1, 5-9)

Thus we gain access to understanding through humility—that is, through a true perception of ourselves in the light of God's mercy. This ladder is climbed in twelve steps: first, cultivating the fear of God; second, understanding that not everything I want is always good for me; third, learning the value of obedience; fourth, learning the power of perseverance; fifth, recognizing one's own sins; sixth, in our trials, seeking rest by remaining with the Lord; seventh, letting ourselves be taught by suffering; eighth, trusting the community; ninth, using words well; tenth, learning the appropriate way of smiling; eleventh, knowing the value of silence; and twelfth, relying only on God's mercy (see RB 7.10-66).

By climbing these twelve steps, we discover a love that overcomes all anxiety and fear. A fruit of humility, this love helps us *intus legere* ("to read inwardly")—that is, to perceive reality beyond appearances, to see things as the Lord sees them (cf. 1 Sam 16:7). The understanding that we reach by way of humility is the truth about ourselves, our total dependence on God's mercy, and consequently the truth about others, also in need of this same mercy. We are therefore called to forgive as we are forgiven, to love as we are loved, to be compassionate and eager to comfort others. In this humility and understanding, we discover the joy that characterizes evangelical happiness: "Blessed are the poor in spirit, for theirs is the kingdom of heaven. Blessed are the meek, for they will inherit the land. Blessed are the merciful, for they will be shown mercy. Blessed are the clean of heart, for they will see God" (Matt 5:3, 5, 7-8). The *Dialogues* of St. Gregory the Great report an episode from the life of Benedict that takes on particular significance in this perspective:

> Long before the night office began, the man of God was standing at his window, where he watched and prayed while the rest were still asleep. In the dead of night he suddenly beheld a flood of light shining down from above more brilliant than the sun, and with it every trace of darkness cleared away. Another remarkable sight followed. According to his own description, the whole world was gathered up before his eyes in what appeared to be a single ray of light. . . . All creation is bound to appear small to a soul that sees the Creator. Once it beholds a little of his light, it finds all creatures small indeed. The light of holy contemplation enlarges and expands the mind in God until it stands above the world.[5]

The frequent portrayal of monastic life as *fuga mundi* ("flight from the world") rightly feeds the suspicions of those who see in it an attitude that is contrary to the Gospels, not in harmony with a Father who so loves the world that he gives his Son for it (cf. John 3:16). So it is significant that for Benedict, the most influential figure of Western monasticism, one's spiritual intelligence—that is, one's ability to "read inwardly" (*intus legere*)—is measured in the capacity to embrace the world, to see it as a whole with the eyes of God. This means that the true monastic never runs away from the world, nor even avoids it, but rather adopts a certain distance with respect to the world *in order to enter into a deeper relationship with it, as from within.* Another way of expressing the same truth is to

5. *St. Gregory the Great: Dialogues*, trans. Odo John Zimmerman, The Fathers of the Church, vol. 39, (Washington, DC: The Catholic University of America Press, 1959), II, 35, 105–106.

say that the monastic brings the world with him, in his heart, and that all the work of self-knowledge leads him to an ever-deeper compassion that extends eventually to the whole of creation.

God's patience

Therefore Benedict, this friend of Wisdom, built a house supported by seven columns—the school of the Lord's service. In this school, the inexperienced are educated to discover the taste of the things of God and the ignorant are taught humility, a deeper knowledge of oneself, of others, and of God. But the fact that wisdom and folly use the exact same words in their calls gives reason for caution: the border between the two is porous, and instead of being nourished with the wine and the bread of wisdom, we can find ourselves with only the water and the bread of folly. On this ambiguity let's express some concluding thoughts.

Our monasteries, as well as our ecclesial communities, too often make promises that they cannot keep. They beckon in the name of wisdom, but they have no experience to offer; they are populated by shadows, by restless and ignorant characters. They invite passersby, but they have no wine to offer; they have only the furtive waters of mediocrity or, worse, hypocrisy. Unfortunately, those who stumble upon them often do not realize this immediately. It takes time to recognize the truth, and it sometimes comes too late—by then, disillusionment or cynicism have already settled into the heart, enthusiasm has been drained, and hope has been corroded.

We can't hide behind a naive conception of God's action in history and believe that even in the most unfavorable circumstances wisdom will play its formative role undisturbed. Of course, this is not impossible, because everything is possible to God. But the reality is that most of the time in such unfortunate conditions, the inexperienced person remains inexperienced and the ignorant person remains ignorant, tragically losing the right path.

We stand before a mystery. The schooling of wisdom involves a fallible human mediation. God takes the risk of using instruments who can mislead people *in his name* instead of leading them along the way of life. It almost seems that folly is part of the risk that wisdom chooses to take. We find two important confirmations of this in Scripture.

First, there is the sad possibility of shepherds who scatter rather than gather their sheep. This is a frequent subject of the Lord's piercing cry of pain in the book of Jeremiah:

> How stupid are the shepherds!
> The LORD they have not sought;
> For this reason they have failed,
> and all their flocks scattered. (Jer 10:21)

The Lord tells Ezekiel, "Son of man, prophesy against the shepherds of Israel. Prophesy and say to them: To the shepherds, thus says the LORD God: Woe to the shepherds of Israel who have been pasturing themselves! Should not shepherds pasture the flock?" (Ezek 34:2).

Second, there is the New Testament vision of the church as a field where both good wheat and useless weeds grow together:

> While everyone was asleep the enemy came and sowed weeds all through the wheat, and then went off. When the crop grew and bore fruit, the weeds appeared as well. The slaves of the householder came to him and said, "Master, did you not sow good seed in your field? Where have the weeds come from?" He answered, "An enemy has done this." His slaves said to him, "Do you want us to go and pull them up?" He replied, "No, if you pull up the weeds you might uproot the wheat along with them. Let them grow together until harvest; then at harvest time I will say to the harvesters, 'First collect the weeds and tie them in bundles for burning; but gather the wheat into my barn.'" (Matt 13:25-30)

Wheat and weeds—wisdom and folly—grow together in the field of the church. This is the Lord's will. It is necessary to allow the weeds to grow in the church: the Lord refuses the untimely zeal of the servants who want to eradicate them immediately. This is one of the most vivid descriptions of the nature and life of the church, reflected on at length by Augustine of Hippo in his polemic against the Donatists and Pelagians. The clear and definitive division between good and evil, wisdom and folly, wheat and weeds is a prerogative that belongs to God alone, and he has reserved it for himself at the end of time. Every attempt to establish a church of the pure, a community of saints, is fatally destined to hypocrisy. The very claim of being able to speak authentically in the name of wisdom, without shadows or equivocations, without at the same time exposing oneself to the tragic possibility of folly, is a sign of inexperience and ignorance.

An adult faith knows it must serenely accept the inevitable mingling of good and evil, wheat and weeds, wisdom and folly in our ecclesial realities, because it knows clearly that the roots of both reach into each of us. The boundary between wisdom and folly is porous in our own hearts, and light and darkness coexist there. Maturity consists not in the illusion of having access to pure and uncontaminated wisdom to offer, but in reconciliation with the ineliminable presence of contradiction and evil in us and with the ever-present risk of folly.

The understanding that comes from humility ultimately consists precisely in this. In all our ecclesial activities, the coexistence of wisdom and folly, the frightening possibility of intending to dispense the former and instead offering the latter, are consequences of God's patience. There is no way forward other than to accept this risk; we must accept it, because God accepts it—and God accepts it because without it, none of us would be saved. The only perfection, the only justice, the only wisdom to which we have access in this age is the Father's mercy and a discernment that must be taken up day after day, tirelessly, until our last breath.

This is the highest manifestation of Benedictine wisdom. It finds expression in the last of the so-called "tools for good works" presented in chapter 4 of the Rule. After a long list of prohibitions and injunctions (ranging from not killing to respecting elders and loving the young), after much advice relating to the ascetic life (to avoid eating too much or sleeping too much or being lazy) and to a truly evangelical community life (not to repay evil for evil; to love one's enemies), the last word, which ultimately underlies all of these instructions, is the following: "And finally, never lose hope in God's mercy" (RB 4.74).

If the boundary between wisdom and folly is porous, if we must deal with the weeds present in our hearts as well as our institutions until the end, then the secret of not losing hope lies in this mercy. Along the way in which we constantly get lost, we know that we can count on the mercy of "the Good Shepherd who left the ninety-nine sheep in the mountains and went in search of the one sheep that had strayed. So great was his compassion for its weakness that he mercifully 'placed it on his' sacred 'shoulders' and so carried it back to the flock" (RB 27.8-9).

CHAPTER II

The Secret of Christian Action

In invocation of God the Father everything depends on whether or not it is done in sheer need (not self-won competence), in sheer readiness to learn (not schooled erudition), and in sheer helplessness (not the application of a technique of self-help). This can be the work only of very weak and very little and very poor children, of those who in their littleness, weakness, and poverty can only get up and run with empty hands to their Father, appealing to him.

Karl Barth[1]

The connection between the monastic vocation and the desert is well known. The first monks, who lived in Egypt in the fourth century, are known as the "desert fathers," and various monastic figures—including Anthony (the father of monasticism) and Benedict—led periods of solitary or eremitic life before founding monasteries or accepting disciples. This link is significant, because it helps us understand not only the meaning of monastic life for

---

1. Karl Barth, *The Christian Life*, Church Dogmatics vol. IV, Part 4, trans. Geoffrey W. Bromiley (London: T&T Clark, 2004), 79–80.

the church but also the meaning of Christian action, *what it means to act in the name of the Lord.*

What can people who choose to leave cities or towns and look for refuge in deserted places offer to the church? Could they not have contributed more by staying in the city, offering to others their vibrant example of Christian living, and continuing along the path of holiness in that context? Christians belonging to denominations that haven't preserved the monastic charism, while respecting and admiring this choice of life, often confess that they don't understand it. They often explain this difficulty by pointing to the mandate that Jesus left to every Christian: "Go, therefore, and make disciples of all nations, baptizing them in the name of the Father, and of the Son, and of the holy Spirit, teaching them to observe all that I have commanded you" (Matt 28:19-20). This seems to suggest that living a Christian life will always mean preaching, teaching, and baptizing others. Only this form of holiness can claim to be evangelical. The Gospel would leave no room for a holiness that consists in withdrawing instead of going forth and being silent instead of teaching.

But this criticism of monastic life hides another question related to the Christian vocation, or more precisely to the logic of Christian action. We know how much the logic of doing, of action, prevails in the modern world. In terms of conditions for the exercise of its mission, Christianity today finds itself in a more favorable context than ever: an abundance of financial resources, technology that makes it possible to contact massive numbers of people quickly and easily, and globalization. Never has the church enjoyed a greater ability to effectively preach, teach, assist those in need and to reach all corners of the earth. This has advantages and drawbacks; it can be judged positively or negatively. But it is a fact; it is our context. And it gives a new urgency to the question of the relationship between God's action and human action, and the question of how to make sure that our action remains the instrument and sign of God's action.

Let us then try to deal theologically with these two questions about the meaning of the monastic vocation and of Christian action, starting with a reflection on the connection that the Gospel makes between baptism, Jesus' action, and the desert. If the desert has an important place in monastic spirituality, it is because in the Gospel it is connected inseparably to baptism and to the action of Jesus.

Becoming children of God

The sequence of the events of Jesus' life presented by the Synoptic Gospels, and especially by Matthew, is significant here. Matthew presents the baptism of Jesus as his manifestation, his "epiphany." We read, "After Jesus was baptized, he came up from the water and behold, the heavens were opened for him, and he saw the Spirit of God descending like a dove and coming upon him. And a voice came from the heavens, saying, 'This is my beloved Son, with whom I am well pleased'" (Matt 3:16-17).

With baptism, Jesus receives his messianic investiture as king, prophet, and priest. He is king because with him comes the kingdom of God; indeed, he is himself the kingdom of God, God who intervenes in a definitive way in history: he *is* the action of God. Then, Jesus is prophet because he speaks in the name of the Lord: he *is* the word of the Lord. Finally, Jesus is priest because he alone offers God fitting worship, worship in spirit and truth, a sacrifice of praise, reconciliation: he *is* peace and reconciliation. Only after this investiture does Jesus begin to exercise his mission of preaching, calling, teaching, proclaiming, and healing:

> From that time on, Jesus began to preach and say, "Repent, for the kingdom of heaven is at hand." As he was walking by the Sea of Galilee, he saw two brothers, Simon who is called Peter, and his brother Andrew, casting a net into the sea; they were fishermen. He said to them, "Come after me, and I will make you fishers of men." At once they left their nets and followed him. He walked along from there and saw two other brothers, James, the son of Zebedee, and his brother John. They were in a boat, with their father Zebedee, mending their nets. *He called them*, and immediately they left their boat and

their father and followed him. He went around all of Galilee, *teaching* in their synagogues, *proclaiming* the gospel of the kingdom, and *curing* every disease and illness among the people. His fame spread to all of Syria, and they brought to him all who were sick with various diseases and racked with pain, those who were possessed, lunatics, and paralytics, and he cured them. And great crowds from Galilee, the Decapolis, Jerusalem, and Judea, and from beyond the Jordan followed him. (Matt 4:17-25, emphasis added)

This activity—summarized in the verbs *calling, teaching, proclaiming*, and *healing*—Jesus continues in the present time. He still calls, teaches, proclaims, and heals, through his Spirit, in the church. He alone converts, he alone reconciles, he alone speaks to our hearts: "I am with you always, until the end of the age" (Matt 28:20). But he wants our action to echo his, reflect his, and point to his. And for this reason, he calls us to preach, teach, proclaim, and heal. In this way, through baptism we, too, become kings, prophets, and priests.

Having said all this, though, we still must grasp a further characteristic of Jesus' activity—the secret, in a certain sense, which really explains its fruitfulness. If we do not decipher this secret, there is an aspect of Christian action that we risk losing sight of, thus compromising its authenticity. If we do not grasp this secret, we can do all the ministry we want and even seem to succeed by producing conspicuous results that inspire admiration, but we build on sand. Activity, success, numerical growth, and public recognition can be merely an appearance; they can be deceiving. In the light of the Gospel, we must try to understand what this secret is, this fundamental characteristic of Jesus' activity, *of God's activity*.

Continuing our reading of the first chapters of Matthew, we see that Jesus' baptism is an epiphany not only because it is the moment we see him authorized to act in the name of the Lord but even more because it reveals the fundamental character of what such action means. In baptism, we do not simply see the Father authorizing Jesus to reign, speak, and reconcile in his name, to preach, teach, heal, convert, work miracles, and cast out demons in his name. In fact, we also witness the revelation of the way, *the only way in which one acts "in the name of the Lord,"* expressed in this sentence from the Father: "This is my beloved Son, with whom I am well pleased" (Matt 3:16-17). The authorization to act in the name of the Lord is not something external, but depends on a quality, an interior attitude: being children, having a filial spirit, the Spirit of the Son (cf. the dove that descends upon Jesus).

Before proceeding further in this analysis, let's recall what we've said previously: the first definition of the monastic given by Benedict in his Rule is precisely that the monastic must be a son or a daughter: "Listen carefully, *my son*, to the master's instructions, and *attend to them with the ear of your heart*. This is advice from a *father* who loves you; welcome it, and faithfully put it into practice. The labor of obedience will bring you back to him from whom you had drifted through the sloth of disobedience" (RB Prol. 1-2, emphasis added).

This initial invitation to listen in the Rule is addressed to a son or a daughter; it is only possible for a son or daughter. For Benedict, the monastic is the one who, in his or her relationship with God, wants to behave as a son/daughter. The meaning of this choice can be found in the succession of events in the Gospel of Matthew that we mentioned above and especially in what Jesus does immediately after this authorization to act in the name of the Lord. Strangely, in fact, we see that he does not immediately begin to preach, call, teach, announce, or heal (cf. Matt 4:17-25)—that is, to *act*. Instead we see that he "was led by the Spirit into the desert" (Matt 4:1-11).

Acting as God

Of course, one might say that this period in the desert is already an *action* of Jesus: he goes to the desert to battle the devil. To establish the kingdom of God, it is necessary to dislodge "the strong man" (Mark 3:27) who has held humanity prisoner. This is why Jesus casts out demons. But that is *not* the way Matthew understands this stage in Jesus' life. The Gospel says: "Then Jesus was led by the Spirit into the desert *to be tempted by the devil*" (Matt 4:1). The period in the desert is about Jesus; it is something that *he* needs in order to begin his mission in the right way, in the right spirit. It is a moment in which he, Jesus, must make a fundamental choice. He has just been proclaimed "Son" (Matt 3:17), but this is still not enough to prepare him to act in the name of the Lord. He wants to act not in the name of a generic God, but of a God whose fundamental identity is to be *Father*. This is why, *before beginning to act*, he must enter into this filial attitude, must make it his own, must choose it. This is the meaning of Christ's temptation by the devil; that story illustrates precisely this point.

The Old Testament presents the desert from two points of view. In some texts, especially in the book of Numbers, it is a place of punishment for the generation of Israelites who put the Lord to the test and did not believe in him: "So the anger of the LORD flared up against the Israelites and he made them wander in the wilderness forty years, until the whole generation that had done evil in the sight of the LORD had disappeared" (Num 32:13).

But in the book of Deuteronomy, the desert is presented as the place of testing (in the sense of verification) and of grace:

> Remember how for these forty years the LORD, your God, has directed all your journeying in the wilderness, *so as to test you by affliction, to know what was in your heart*: to keep his commandments, or not. He therefore let you be afflicted with hunger, and then fed you with manna, a food unknown to you and your ancestors, *so you might know that it is not by bread alone that people live, but by all that comes forth from the mouth of the LORD.* The clothing did not fall from you in tatters, nor did your feet swell these forty years. (Deut 8:2-4, emphasis added)

Here the desert is where people experience their own poverty and their total dependence on the Lord. The aim of this experience is to help them discover the absolute fidelity of the Lord, who never lets his people lack what they need. The desert is where the Lord teaches his people how to be in relationship with him, but also tests them, "to know what is in their hearts" (cf. Deut 8:2). The parallel between Jesus' forty days and Israel's forty years in the desert is unmistakable and intentional. Jesus' experience, however, does not include the dimension of punishment emphasized by the book of Numbers, but only Deuteronomy's dimension of testing and the unveiling of what is in one's heart. The way the devil tempts Jesus makes this clear: "If you are the Son of God, command that these stones become loaves of bread" and "If you are the Son of God, throw yourself down" (Matt 4:3, 6). These temptations focus on what it means to be a child of God, on what it means to act ("command," "throw," and so on) in the name of God, on what it means to act as God.

This is why the desert is the crucial transition between Jesus' authorization to act in the name of the Lord and the actual beginning of his activity. It is not enough to be invested with a mission, an authority, a vocation to ensure that God works through our action—that he establishes his kingdom (not ours), fulfills his will (not ours), sanctifies his name (not ours). This sojourn in the desert must first lay bare what we have in our hearts, unmask the fundamental temptation that is in them and to which none of us will ever be able to escape completely, which is to take possession of the mission received from the Father and to exercise it autonomously, independently.

Jesus, the Son of God who later, in the multiplication of the loaves, made bread appear out of nothing, certainly had the authority and the power to transform stones into bread; he who walked on water could certainly have thrown himself down from the pinnacle of the Temple and flown; and he who was God had every right to be served by angels. And for the devil, all this was precisely what it meant to be the Son of God, to act in the name of the Lord, to "act as God." But what Satan does not understand, what the logic of the world does not understand, what our hearts left to themselves cannot understand is what it really means to be children of the Father, what it really is to act as children of the Father.

Bypassing the desert

Let us pause here to better understand why this reflection is important and relevant. Why—despite an abundance of financial and technological means, numerical strength, and enormous institutional weight—is the witness of Christianity, and Catholicism in particular, in the midst of such a serious crisis today? Why has it become so difficult to encounter the Father through the witness and mission of the church?

In the light of the Gospel, the answer is clear. It is because the church's action and mission overlook their necessary *rootedness in the desert*. It is because our conception of authority, mission, and action is the same as that of Satan, who says to Jesus, "What are you waiting for? You have a mission, you have authority—so act!" Or worse still, it is because, enthralled by the seduction of power (financial, political, or even the prestige that, despite everything, the institution still in some ways enjoys), we do not know how to answer like Jesus: "The Lord, your God, shall you worship / and him alone shall you serve" (Matt 4:10).

Our sins against this truth are usually not ones of commission—that is, intentionally and consciously embracing the logic of Satan and the world—but, above all, sins of omission. And this is the key here. The idols of activism, autonomy, power, success, and prestige are in everyone's hearts. No one is completely immune from them. Our sin is not in having these idols in our hearts or in being conditioned by them in the exercise of our mission. Our sin is in neglecting the need to pass through the desert before acting, in order to unmask these idols that hold our hearts prisoner and threaten to push us to ignore the logic of God in favor of the logic of Satan ("If you are the Son of God, command . . . throw yourself down . . ."). Our sin is an omission, because we do not give ourselves the time to integrate the desert into our spiritual life; we do not allow what is in our hearts to be revealed to us. Only through the desert, in fact, can we stop deluding ourselves about the authenticity of our intentions and enter the process of self-knowledge that is part of any authentic spirituality.

Saved by failure

What, then, is the logic of God, of God's kingdom, and God's will? Let us carefully review the succession of events in the Gospel of Matthew: first is the baptism of Jesus (Matt 3:13-17), then the desert (Matt 4:1-11), then the beginning of Jesus' activity (Matt 4:12-25), and finally his first discourse, the beatitudes (Matt 5–7).

The beatitudes—the Magna Carta of Christianity— must be read in the light of Jesus' sojourn in the desert. The entire Sermon on the Mount (the context of the beatitudes) can be summarized in the phrase, "that you may be *children* of your heavenly Father" (Matt 5:45). In the desert, Jesus responds to the devil's distorted understanding of what it means to be a child of God ("if you are the Son of God") through answers and actions that show what it really means to be "Son of God." Then, in the beatitudes, he explains it further. We will examine two of these explanations in particular: "Blessed are the poor in spirit, for theirs is the kingdom of heaven" (Matt 5:3) and the Our Father (Matt 6:9-13). (In fact, we might interpret chapters 5 through 7 as the case that holds the precious pearl that is the Our Father.)

To be children, to act as children, is to be poor in spirit. The devil says to Jesus, in effect, "Show that you're the Son of God by feeding yourself," and Jesus replies, "In reality I show that I am truly Son if I entrust myself to the Father, if I await the moment in which he will decide to feed me, because I know he takes care of me." The Son knows he is at the service of a mission, a will, a salvation, and a kingdom that is not his, but precisely God's, and for this he knows that the most important way to *act* is to pray, hope, believe, and wait—this is the meaning of being poor in spirit. We see this when he says "Give us this day our daily bread" (Matt

6:11) and "One does not live by bread alone, / but by every word that comes forth from the mouth of God" (Matt 4:4) and "Do not worry and say, 'What are we to eat?' or 'What are we to drink?' or 'What are we to wear?' All these things the pagans seek. Your heavenly Father knows that you need them all. But seek first the kingdom of God and his righteousness, and all these things will be given you besides" (Matt 6:31-33).

And indeed, at the end of the story of Jesus' temptation, we see that the Father takes care of Jesus, sending his angels to feed him (cf. Matt 4:11).

We see this idea again in the way Jesus responds to his disciples when they want to wield the sword to defend him: "Put your sword back into its sheath, for all who take the sword will perish by the sword. Do you think that I cannot call upon my Father and he will not provide me at this moment with more than twelve legions of angels?" (Matt 26:52-53). And the same temptation comes back to Jesus when he is on the cross:

> Those passing by reviled him, shaking their heads and saying, "You who would destroy the temple and rebuild it in three days, save yourself, if you are the Son of God, and come down from the cross!" Likewise the chief priests with the scribes and elders mocked him and said, "He saved others; he cannot save himself. So he is the king of Israel! Let him come down from the cross now, and we will believe in him. He trusted in God; let him deliver him now if he wants him. For he said, 'I am the Son of God.'" (Matt 27:40-43)

Always the same provocation: "If you are a Son, if you really have power, do it yourself." Instead, Jesus, by his actions, replies: "On the contrary, I show that I am a Son by allowing the Father to act, precisely by continuing to believe and hope in him against all hope." This is how Jesus saves us.

We can paradoxically say that it is not Jesus' activity, not his "success," that saved us. His preaching had some success at the beginning, but in the end it was not enough to create a sufficiently influential movement to resist the power of his opponents. The people he had chosen to support him turned out to be unsuitable; they couldn't keep watch with him even for an hour, didn't understand his words, continued to quarrel with each other for the first place until the end, denied him, and then vanished at the hour of his death. What saved us is what appeared, in the eyes of the world, to be Jesus' failure, the demonstration of his total powerlessness—that is, his waiting for the Father to act, to take his defense, to confirm with the resurrection what he had proclaimed at Jesus' baptism: "You are my Son." What saved us was Jesus' poverty in spirit.

Poverty in spirit

The place where Jesus gave this fundamental orientation to his action, where he learned poverty in spirit, was the desert. And in doing so, he showed us that the desert is the foundation of our identity as Christians, as daughters and sons of the Father guided by the Spirit, and the foundation of our mission to lead, speak, and reconcile in the name of the Father, whatever form this then assumes.

The desert is where we discover "what is in our hearts" (cf. Deut 8:2)—that is, the self-knowledge that is the basis of monastic and Christian asceticism, the acknowledgment of our sin, humility, poverty in spirit: there are so many ways to describe this foundation, but the substance is the same. It is a matter of understanding that, left to ourselves, we inevitably play Satan's game, and we adopt the logic of the world: "Do not love the world or the things of the world. If anyone loves the world, the love of the Father is not in him. For all that is in the world, sensual lust, enticement for the eyes, and a pretentious life, is not from the Father but is from the world. Yet the world and its enticement are passing away. But whoever does the will of God remains forever" (1 John 2:15-17).

The desert is where we learn what it means truly to be children of God. It is where we learn to pray the Our Father truthfully. Progress in the spiritual life is measured by the truth with which we say the Our Father—not only with our lips, but with our lives.

And finally, the desert is the place to which Jesus constantly returns in the course of his mission, every time we see him retire to a solitary place to pray. In a similar way, we, too, must constantly integrate the experience of the desert in our spiritual life.

Embracing the desert

In conclusion, we must ask ourselves how one concretely experiences the desert in Christian life today.

On the one hand, there is the experience of the desert imposed by the circumstances of life—the trials, moments of failure, periods of weakness (illness, misunderstandings, and so on). These are the moments in which, whether we want it or not, we are reduced to impotence and can only wait for salvation to come from the Lord. And often we discover in hindsight that these were the periods of greatest fruitfulness in our lives. This experience finds expression in the beautiful prayer of Psalm 119: "I look for your salvation, Lord" (Ps 119:166).

But the desert that constitutes the foundation of our spiritual life is, above all, something we can choose, and it consists in prayer and self-knowledge.

The fundamental reason for the crisis that monasticism and Christianity are currently experiencing is that Christians, including monastics, have ceased to be men and women of prayer. It is not a question, of course, of underestimating the importance of the *opus Dei*, of the communal celebration of the liturgy, which will be discussed later. But to reduce prayer to its communal, liturgical celebration is precisely what inevitably makes it sterile and is the profound reason for the painful ritualizing, aestheticizing, and clericalist drift that has characterized much understanding of the liturgy in recent years and from which, by God's grace, we may now be emerging.

Jesus participated in the prayer of the synagogue and recited the psalms in common with his disciples; this was the foundation of his prayer life. But repeatedly, he went away by himself before sunrise to pray. He knew that the experience of the desert at the beginning of his ministry had to be renewed constantly, every day. His silent prayer in the presence of the Father was his way of making sure that the desert—the filial attitude, the unveiling of what was in his heart—remained, continuously and actively, at the foundation of his ministry and his action. This is why he was so strict in warning his disciples with words that we can paraphrase as follows:

> Do not think that prayer is standing in the churches to be seen by people, multiplying liturgical formulas, hymns, psalms, and words. This can become a form of hypocrisy! If you want to be sure of encountering the Father, go into your room, close the door, and pray to him in the secret of your heart (and of course, then your prayer in the synagogue will also be protected from hypocrisy, so as to express this relationship with the Father).[2]

But there are many other possible actualizations of the desert in our monastic life, our community life, and the Christian life. The desert is also the habitual distance that we preserve with respect to our action, words, decisions, and convictions; it is the usual distance necessary for constant verification, constant discernment.

Let's take the example of meetings about any type of decision that concerns the life of the community or of the church. The basic intention of seeking God's will is not enough to make sure we find it. It is inevitable that other dynamics that hinder this freedom and this discernment will furtively come into play. We are in fact

---

2. This is my paraphrase of Matthew 6:5-7, which reads: "When you pray, do not be like the hypocrites, who love to stand and pray in the synagogues and on street corners so that others may see them. Amen, I say to you, they have received their reward. But when you pray, go to your inner room, close the door, and pray to your Father in secret. And your Father who sees in secret will repay you. In praying, do not babble like the pagans, who think that they will be heard because of their many words."

constantly at the mercy of our passions, our fears, our egos, and all of these inevitably condition the way we try to have community discussions and make decisions, to the point that, almost without wanting to, we begin to impose ourselves with force, using pressure or influence that may be legitimate in a political arena, but which has no place in the context of authentically Christian community discernment.

To be and remain Christian, community discernment can never be about seeking the coming of *my* kingdom and the fulfillment of *my* will, but about the coming of *God's* kingdom and the fulfillment of *God's* will.

That these deviations should be part of the life of the church at all levels is normal; this is in our hearts, and it is useless to be under any illusions. Here, too, our sin lies not in the presence of such inclinations in our hearts, nor in the fact that they always end up conditioning our actions. Our sin is, rather, once again one of omission: we do not take the precautions that would help us avoid being guided by these inclinations. We bypass the desert, elude the work necessary to become aware of what we have in our hearts. In this case, among other things, the desert means praying during meetings and between meetings, not just formally, but truly, so that we are sure of maintaining a filial attitude, just as Jesus, before his decision-making, withdrew to the desert to pray. If he needed it, how much more do we?

CHAPTER III

Eager for Trials

What Benedict is interested in producing is people who have the skills to diagnose everything inside them that prompts them to escape from themselves in the here and now.

Rowan Williams[1]

One of the most important sentences of the Rule of Benedict is found in the chapter on the acceptance of new brothers and sisters into the community: "The concern must be whether the novice truly seeks God and whether he [or she] shows eagerness for the Work of God, for obedience and for trials" (RB 58.7). Without a doubt, seeking God, the liturgy, and obedience are dear to anyone who finds nourishment in the spirituality of the Rule. But what about the "eagerness for trials" Benedict mentions here? The expression is even more unsettling in Latin, because the word here translated as "trials" is *obprobria*. We associate this with the English word opprobrium, which means "vilification" and the shame associated with it. We say of people who have done something shameful that they "deserve opprobrium" or that they have "public opprobrium heaped upon" them—negative connotations

1. Williams, *The Way of St Benedict*, 22.

that no healthy spirituality could ever endorse. Translators of the Rule have often rendered this term in English as "humiliations."

The surest criterion for determining the meaning of a word is always internal—that is, to piece together the meaning of the word from its context. In the paragraph in which *obprobria* appears, its meaning can be discerned from the following sentence, with its reference to "hardships and difficulties that will lead [the monastic] to God" (RB 58.8). Translating it as "trials" would seem most accurate, then, and, in light of the fourth step of humility described in chapter seven of the same Rule, it can be identified with the evangelical attitude described in the Sermon on the Mount and in parallel passages of the New Testament: "In truth, those who are patient amid hardships and unjust treatment are fulfilling the Lord's command: 'When struck on one cheek, they turn the other; when deprived of their coat, they offer their cloak also; when pressed into service for one mile, they go two' (Matt 5:39-41). With the Apostle Paul, they bear with 'false brothers,' 'endure persecution,' and 'bless those who curse them' (2 Cor 11:26; 1 Cor 4:12)" (RB 7.42-43; cf. also Luke 6:29).

In other words, the evangelical response to trials is not passivity, but a greater commitment to relationship. One does not offer the other cheek or travel the extra mile as some kind of self-punishment, a need to be humiliated by one's adversary, but as an expression of unshakable trust in the possibility of the enemy's conversion and as a constant willingness to be creative in the search for ever-new ways to understand the other and reach out to the other in his or her suffering. The eagerness for trials to which Benedict calls us, interpreted in the light of the Gospel, is therefore an invitation to explore a whole range of imaginative responses to the inevitable difficulties that are encountered on the path that leads to God.

Three such ways of responding creatively to trials will guide us in this reflection. The first positive response to trials is *readiness*, or in the Latin text, *sollicitudo* (RB 58.7). Linking it with the fourth step of humility in the seventh chapter of the Rule, this *sollicitudo* becomes patience, perseverance, endurance (RB 7.35-43). The second positive response is the one suggested by the Gospel's hyperbole, "turn the other cheek." It encapsulates the overall spirit of the Sermon on the Mount in the Gospel of Matthew (RB 7.42-43; cf. Matt 5–7). Finally, the third healthy response to setbacks is that of *guidance*. The role of the guide or formator is expressed in a few sentences, very dense with meaning, in chapter 58 of the Rule, but it symbolically represents the entirety of monastic training and includes recourse to the word of God as a criterion for deciphering and guiding spiritual life, as can be seen from the collage of biblical quotations, each carefully chosen, that these passages include.

It is necessary, then, to show, not only from a theoretical point of view but also from a concrete one, based on experience, how these three ways of responding allow trials (*obprobria*) to become testing; meaningless suffering to be transfigured in the "cross"—that is, in suffering that brings salvation; and finally, mortification and self-emptying to become an opportunity for growth—not only spiritual growth, but also human, emotional, and psychological growth.

Ongoing testing

The period of novitiate is presented by Benedict's Rule as a time of *probatio*, testing, in the Johannine sense of the term: "Test the spirits to see whether they belong to God" (1 John 4:1). It is a matter of the novice being "tested in patience" (RB 58.11). As the quality of glass is judged by its transparency, so the inspirations and thoughts of the heart are confirmed through principles developed by monastic wisdom. And it is not just a matter of confirming the fundamental inspiration that leads a young person to the monastery, which we commonly call "vocation," but also all the smaller inspirations that guide various choices along the path of following Christ. This is why Benedict describes not only the novitiate but the entire monastic life as a *diuturna probatio*, a "lasting test" (RB 1.3),[2] in the sense of an ongoing verification and discernment.

---

2. RB1980 renders it as "the test of living in a monastery for a long time."

Benedict ascribes this *probatio*, this testing, to two primary agents: God and the spiritual guide.

The seventh chapter of the Rule, on humility, tells us that the one who puts us to the test, who purifies us, is first of all the Lord himself: "O God, you have tested us, you have tried us as silver is tried by fire; you have led us into a snare, you have placed afflictions on our backs" (RB 7.40, quoting Ps 66:10-11). In the psalm quoted here, the purpose of the *probatio* is to lead people to entrust themselves solely to the Lord. It refers to the famous episode of the book of Exodus, just before the miracle of the Red Sea, when God's people find themselves trapped between the Egyptian army and an uncrossable stretch of sea.

Such *probatio* is part of the Lord's education and is intended to teach us patience and endurance, *hypomoné*, one of the most important Christian virtues in the New Testament—"Whoever endures to the end will be saved" (Matt 10:22)—also recommended in the Letter to the Hebrews:

> You need endurance to do the will of God and receive what he has promised. . . . Therefore, since we are surrounded by so great a cloud of witnesses, let us rid ourselves of every burden and sin that clings to us and persevere in running the race that lies before us while keeping our eyes fixed on Jesus, the leader and perfecter of faith. . . . Consider how he endured such opposition from sinners, in order that you may not grow weary and lose heart. In your struggle against sin you have not yet resisted to the point of shedding blood. (Heb 10:36; 12:1-4)

Paul points to the link between perseverance and *probatio* in his letter to the Romans, when he states that "endurance [*hypomoné*] [produces] proven character [*dokimé*]" (Rom 5:4)— the former confirms the latter. And in turn this proven character confirms that love has been poured into our hearts through the Holy Spirit who has been given to us (cf. Rom 5:5). That is why patience is not something to be endured with resignation, but to be embraced (cf.

RB 7.42). Furthermore, it is important to note that, for Benedict, the object of this *probatio* is the values of the Gospel: the invitation to turn the other cheek, to give one's tunic also, to travel two miles with those who force us to go one, to forgive our enemies (RB 7.42; cf. Matt 5:39-48).

To speak of a second agent of *probatio* alongside God is, of course, improper. We do it only from the textual point of view in order to illustrate the education proposed by the Rule of Benedict for administering *probatio*. Too many abuses were committed in the not-too-distant past against young people by formators in the name of "testing," where an arbitrary conception of obedience prevailed, and spirituality was marked by anthropological pessimism. These abuses often involved the violation of the private sphere, which always carries serious risks of manipulation. It's enough to recall practices like intercepting and reading a novice's mail, dictating which priest a novice may confess to, or the use of nonprofessional psychological tools—the list could go on. Behind each of these deviations was an arbitrary conception of *probatio*, as if it were a technique to wear down the novices' resistance, bend their will, and push them to renounce their own personality.

The only authentically evangelical form of *probatio* is one that the formators or guides practice in their own lives as an ongoing confirmation of their own inspirations through a constant contact with the word of God in prayer. Only those who live such a *probatio* will succeed in not simply putting novices to the test, but gradually teaching them to be the agents of their own *probatio*. It is an education in self-verification and self-discernment.

In 1 John, the unmistakable sign of belonging to God is what John calls "the anointing": "You have the anointing that comes from the holy one, and you all have knowledge" (1 John 2:20). If a person needs constantly to be tended by someone else, it means she lacks the understanding that ought to be hers as a Christian and that the formation process has failed. In the Christian context, formation and accompaniment have value only to the extent that they bring people into contact with the interior anointing, only if they teach them how to let themselves be guided and instructed by the Spirit present in their own hearts: "As for you, the anointing that you received from him remains in you, so that you do not need anyone to teach you. But his anointing teaches you about everything and is true and not false; just as it taught you, remain in him" (1 John 2:27).

It is not therefore a matter of the formator putting the novices to the test, but of helping them to become aware of the inspirations, desires, impulses, and instincts that motivate them, so that they become able to understand for themselves which of these are rooted in the Gospel and which are not, which correspond to the presence and action of the Spirit in their heart and which are simply whims.

The role of the young person in formation is therefore anything but passive. Benedict's vocabulary suggests a great dynamism, above all, through his use of the word *sollicitus*: it is necessary to verify whether the novice "shows eagerness [*sollicitus*] for the Work of God, for obedience and for trials" (RB 58.7). Etymologically *sollicitus* comes from *sollus*, "entire," and *citus*, "in movement"; that is, it is a question of the novice being "entirely in motion." We see the same idea in the phrase *noviter veniens quis ad conversationem*, whose accusative also suggests direction and movement and can be adequately translated only by paraphrase, such as "the newcomers who join the constant movement of conversion which is monastic life" (cf. RB 58.1). And indeed, the evangelical conception of conversion is one of continuous movement. What does Jesus enjoin to those he calls to conversion? To follow him. To "come after me" (Mark 1:17). And we know that Jesus does not have even a stone where he can lay his head because he is always on the move; he cannot stop anywhere except the bosom of the Father to whom he returns, carrying upon his own shoulders the lost sheep.

Probatio is therefore only one more description of monastic life. It must be interpreted in accordance with the idea of movement that emerges everywhere in Benedict's Rule and is effectively summarized at the end of the prologue, which speaks of the constant "overflowing" of the heart that happens thanks to ongoing "progress in the way of life and faith" with a tempo that must express eagerness from the beginning and that is destined to progressively become a race: "We shall run on the path of God's commandments, our hearts overflowing with the inexpressible delight of love" (RB Prol. 49).

Trials and verification

So what is the relationship between *trials* (*obprobria*)—that is, as we have said, all the "hardships and difficulties" that one encounters in monastic life—and the *testing* (*probatio*) through which one grows in the right relationships with God and with oneself? Above all, how do trials become testing?

If we reflect on the nature of the trials that one inevitably encounters in community life, we realize that they are not only or even primarily what is outwardly hard, harsh, difficult, or ungratifying; this is not enough to make them *obprobria* in the sense that Benedict gives to this word. After all, the very same things that trouble some people leave others unmoved; things that exasperate some are borne cheerfully by others. They become trials because of how we perceive them from within. A difficult or unpleasant thing becomes a trial when it causes exasperation, depression, frustration, when it makes one sad, grumpy, dark, or wanting to run away.

Consequently, this is one of the fundamental ways in which trials are turned into testing: external events, the framework of life, the people we live with remain the same; what changes is our interior attitude, which shifts from being negative to positive. It is the process advocated by Paul when he urges us to remove "all bitterness, fury, [and] anger" (Eph 4:31) and to welcome the fruits of the Holy Spirit: "love, joy, peace, patience, kindness, generosity, faithfulness, gentleness, self-control" (Gal 5:22-23).

To illustrate this process, we begin by considering the "bitterness, fury, [and] anger" Paul speaks of. Anger is a powerful emotion and certainly a great challenge in the process of human and emotional maturation for every person and especially for community living.

Anger never lies

It is not uncommon for young monastics, after one or two years of community life, to have the impression of having become worse than they were before entering the monastery: they feel cold inside, unable to pray, besieged by obsessive thoughts of envy, jealousy, or by anxiety. They regret being involved in unhealthy conflicts on often insignificant issues. There may be headaches, nervousness, irritability, and a heavy sense of guilt.

While the manifestations of this malaise are multiple, its root is singular. Common life is a sort of acid test that never fails to expose the unresolved tensions of our heart and we might feel threatened by the aspects of our personality that we are unable to hide any longer. This can trigger a survival mechanism similar to what an animal feels when it is in danger, and anger appears. But since we have been taught to feel guilty about anger, we try to suppress it by internalizing it, and by doing so, we risk wasting all the positive energy it bears.

A fundamental principle of anger management is expressed in the maxim "Anger never lies." Anger is an indicator, an instinctive response, not an enemy or arbitrary experience. If we feel anger, there is always a reason that is often not the one we immediately think about. Most of the time, what we consider to be the cause of our anger is simply the *occasion* for it. This is why anger must be taken seriously. It must be considered carefully, faced serenely, scrutinized—in a word, it must be *honored*.

If Benedict had written his Rule today, in a post-Freudian world, one item he might have included in his list of tools for good works (in chapter 4) is the principle "Honor your anger."

The first and perhaps most serious temptation to avoid in this is to "spiritualize" one's anger prematurely—for example, by feeling guilty about it or by deceiving oneself that it can be dispelled by turning the other cheek or through prayer. This is not a question of denying the work of grace, of course, but of recognizing that the Holy Spirit respects the rhythms of human and emotional growth and, rather than magically resolving it, accompanies the travail and growth with his consolation.

Spiritualizing anger prematurely can become an unconscious means of repression. The anger may seem to disappear, but in fact its external manifestation has only been suppressed, while it continues to live internally, to "eat away inside us." This phenomenon is the source of many somatizations (when psychological concerns manifest themselves as physical symptoms), some of which are more or less harmless (headaches, backaches, dermatitis, heartburn, and so on), while others are, in the long run, much more serious and capable of generating illness and disease that can even lead to death. Anger never lies, and it is counterproductive to try to force it to keep quiet. When we suppress the external manifestations, the body will find a way to speak.

Anyone who has had even minimal experience as a formator knows these mechanisms well and has learned to be very suspicious of angelic behavior—that is, personalities who behave impeccably and keep everything under control. The well-known novel by Robert Louis Stevenson, *The Strange Case of Dr. Jekyll and Mr. Hyde*, holds the esteemed place it does precisely because it illustrates so perfectly this constitutive aspect of human nature: there is within each of us the positive and the negative, the angel and the beast, generosity and selfishness. Maturity does not mean the elimination of one of the two parts, but the integration of both.

This is a typical part of all human life and growth. But it becomes particularly acute in the religious or monastic context, because nothing more than the sacred can become an alibi and a refuge for "angelism," the pretention that the anarchic or instinctive parts of our personality can be brought under control or erased.

However, it is always wrong to blame ourselves for these behaviors. Guilt is just another symptom of the same phenomenon, just another of the many heads of the idolatrous hydra we mentioned above, another of the ways we suppress anger by absorbing it and directing it against ourselves. It is wrong to feel guilty about anger, because the issue is not primarily a moral one; it is not a matter of the will. No one can simply choose not to be angry, as though the anger would then disappear. Instead, anger should be welcomed as an invitation to understand ourselves better, to reach the root of problems. Anger, as we said, never lies; it reveals the need to face unresolved issues that each of us carries within ourselves, a process that the spiritual tradition has called *self-knowledge*. This brings us back to what we said about *probatio*, the testing of motivations for our actions and decisions and, we could add, of our instincts and passions: this testing is the expression of the eagerness required by Benedict, that is the creative dynamism we need to deal well with trials.

Nothing determines the success or failure of living monastic life as much as whether one masters the complex and demanding art of *attende tibi ipse*, taking care of oneself, paying attention to oneself in the form of self-knowledge. Emotions must be given attention. Instincts must be welcomed. Jealousies, envy, and grudges must not be feared or blamed but faced honestly. The body must be appreciated. The past must be examined to identify which aspects of our lives we need to resolve and come to terms with. One's frustrations must be recognized and accepted. We must be clear about what leads us to act, what motivates us. In a word, it is necessary to become familiar with the beast that dwells in us.

A helpful image in this regard could be this: If you were locked in a room and you knew there was a dangerous Doberman there with you, would you turn your back on the dog and ignore it, hoping that if you pretend it doesn't exist it will leave you alone? Wouldn't you rather choose to keep an eye on it, follow its movements, monitoring exactly where it is and what it is doing, ready to respond to any threat? And wouldn't this approach be the only one that offered any hope of living with this troublesome guest and maybe even learning how to tame it?

Generations of monks and nuns have spent their lives consumed by frustrations, unhealthy resentments, bitterness, and regrets for not having been initiated to this essential work of self-knowledge. Many have managed to arrive at this self-knowledge only during mid-life crises, sometimes with the help of professional psychological counseling. So much suffering, depression, sadness, and conflict might have been mitigated if this work of self-knowledge had been undertaken in the early years of formation.

Regression

One needn't be a professional psychologist to recognize some of the typical dynamics of the initial period of monastic formation.[3] At the beginning of religious life, as well as at other important stages, a common experience is the phenomenon of *regression*. Old impulses and feelings connected to the early years of life—such as jealousies, rivalries, a need for attention, and fears—begin to resurface. Important aspects of one's relationship with one's parents, especially what was unresolved and thought to be left in the past, are relived.

To experience such regression is a good sign, because the instinctive part of ourselves can become manifest only in a context where we feel like we're free to be ourselves and accepted for who we are. When we're not sure of being loved, we maintain a facade and present ourselves as an angel. Only when we feel sufficiently safe can we also allow the less flattering aspects of our personality to be seen. The challenge in the context of formation is to make sure young people have the freedom to express themselves and that they are taught how to address aspects of their past that negatively affect the present. In the face of such old and unresolved issues, we are all oftentimes victims of mechanisms of repetition. Until we discover different ways of reacting, we simply relive the same failures, frustrations, and conditionings. In short, regression, if managed well, can become a fundamental opportunity for healing.

3. For many of these thoughts I rely on countless insightful and stimulating conversations with the psychoanalyst Geneviève de Taisne, lecturer at the Catholic Institute of Paris.

Monastic wisdom has developed such an elaborate framework of initial formation because it began to understand such mechanisms and how to deal positively with them long before modern psychology shed light on them. The period of formation is a transitional phase. It is a time of giving up some old ways and gradually appropriating a new way of being. Every transition generates anxiety because it reminds us of our mortality. To renounce professional success, biological fruitfulness, and complete freedom to determine one's own destiny are forms of death that inevitably cause suffering. But such renunciations, such death, can be the prelude to a deeper and more authentic life.

The fact that we freely choose monastic life does not protect us from the distress this journey involves. Even Christ himself, who had freely chosen to embrace the passion, was not spared anguish in living it. There was nothing attractive about the cross. For the Roman soldiers, it was a banal task, carried out expeditiously, involving none of the symbolic dramatization presented in the Gospels. Finding oneself alone and brutalized cannot but cast doubt on the sense of what one is doing. Similarly, the death represented by the transition experienced in the process of monastic formation cannot fail to have an impact on one's psychology, body, and health. It is a real death, of the kind Paul himself wrote about: "We know that our old self was crucified with him" (Rom 6:6).

This distress generates a stream of negative thoughts that must be processed, addressed, and managed. Management of these thoughts is the main challenge of the first years of formation, and a frank relationship of the young person with his or her formator is the fundamental place for this to start. We will never be completely free of negative thoughts; they will always be ready to rise again in moments of conflict or crisis. Initiation into monastic and spiritual life teaches us not to be alone with our own thoughts, but to examine them in the presence of God, in the light of the Gospel. It is especially the relationship with God in prayer that allows us to have the necessary distance to avoid being overwhelmed by the waves of negative thoughts.

It is always risky to try to provide a simplified version of the complex psychological processes we experience. Nothing replaces the benefits of professional psychological accompaniment when we find ourselves at the mercy of difficulties that imprison us. Access to a therapist must be available in every authentic formation program, should be entirely free, and it must be clearly separated from spiritual direction. The formator should never intrude on the work that a young person in formation does with a therapist; she must remain in her own role and let the results of psychological work manifest themselves with time. The confusion of psychological and spiritual accompaniment has too often led to devastating forms of manipulation. But we will return to this point. For now, it is important to note this distinction to contextualize the reflections that follow.

The formator is not a therapist and must actively avoid the temptation to come to easy conclusions about the unconscious mechanisms that determine the behavior of people in formation. On the other hand, though, she must not ignore some of these mechanisms in order to remain humble, to avoid any easy spiritualization of the difficulties and their possible solutions, and above all to understand the different factors that condition the behavior of the people entrusted to her.

One way of understanding these factors, maybe simplistic but still useful, is to realize that each of us carries within ourselves a side that we might call "father/mother" and a side we could call "child." The "father/mother" side is that which developed in us as a result of the education we received. These are rules we have internalized, models that consciously or not inspire our actions (often based on how our own father or mother would behave), the expectations of our parents and all those who helped make us who we are. It is by such expectations that we measure the value of what we do. Meanwhile, the "child" aspect is what we feel instinctively. It is pure energy, the engine that feeds the totality of our being—the need to be desired, seen, listened to by someone in order to exist. It is the confidence necessary to overcome challenges, as well as our tastes, deep desires, and everything that gives us not only pleasure but true and profound joy.

The joys we have internalized from the relationship with our parents can constitute, we know, one of the greatest strengths in life. But each of us must also inevitably deal with the pain of that relationship and its impact on our lives. Often this very pain, the wounds we carry within, lead us into conflict with the "father/mother" side of our personality, leaving us unable to deal constructively with our drives, and so to become slaves to them. At other times, we can encounter the opposite tendency—identification with the expectations of our parents, or at least with those we have internalized, to the point that the "child" aspect of our personality is stifled. We then lose contact with what we feel, with the instinctive aspect of who we are, with our psychic energy, with our living selves. This can happen to the point of denying our own desires, tastes, instincts, and whatever gives us joy and pleasure. We live only by rules and are slaves of what we think others expect of us. We live and make choices by force of will. But losing contact with our most life-giving passions and desires means we deplete our vital energy and never restore it, so that at a certain point we find ourselves empty, unable to move forward, without strength, without motivation.

Having reached such a place, we can sink into depression or rebel against this mechanism through behaviors that seem purely selfish. It is always a grace when, instead of depression, there is a kind of interior rebellion, because it means we have put ourselves back in touch with our "child" side—that is, with the source of our energy. We needn't be bewildered by the egocentric or restless behaviors that come out in these situations. We rediscover our need for attention, to be heard, in order to listen to the part of ourselves that we've ignored for too long. We rediscover the need to ask ourselves, "What do I really want? Who am I? Where do I want to go with my life?"

These dynamics are active not only on a personal level but also on a social one. It is hard to deny that our society is dominated today by the "child" side—there is nothing anyone can't or shouldn't do, the world seems more virtual than real, and making choices becomes ever more difficult. But at the same time, no one really wants to go back to the times when real impulses and needs were suppressed by authority or by predefined models that imprisoned existence solely in duty. The naive and extreme explosion of impulses and rejection of authority of the late 1960s was the reawakening of the "child" side on a social level and, while this brought difficulties and problems, it also made us aware of the need for authority to acknowledge and respect instinctive drives and needs. Crises—both personal and social—are inevitable. We needn't fear them or try to prevent them; they are part of life, and they are indispensable opportunities for growth and maturation.

It is precisely such maturation that we should now pause to consider in more detail. In the light of our reflections to this point, we will consider this maturation in terms of *unification*.

We reach a certain maturity when the two sides of our personality that we have outlined so far are assumed and integrated, despite—or thanks to—the tension that exists between them. Establishing an equilibrium between the disciplined part (the "father/mother" side) and the drives (the "child" side) is possible only thanks to a certain fluidity, the ability to preserve one without denying the other, to know when to grant concessions to one without ignoring the other. This requires a healthy realism, a dynamic tension that is never resolved once and for all, but is negotiated unceasingly. The opposite of this dynamic tension is cutting off, denying, and rejecting a part of ourselves—*splitting*. In this light, we can take up the three ways of responding creatively to the trials that we noted above, namely eagerness (*sollicitudo*), turning the other cheek, and the role of the guide.

Being in motion

Here we find again the importance of the dynamism and fluidity suggested by Benedict's vocabulary, especially through the use of *sollicitus* in the chapter of the Rule on formation—it is necessary to verify that the novice "shows eagerness [that is, is entirely in motion] for the Work of God, for obedience and for trials" (RB 58.7). From the beginning, the young person must be formed not to delude himself or herself about the true nature of maturity. We don't achieve it by killing the beast in us, but through an ever-deeper and more authentic acceptance of ourselves, an ever more generous love of self, made possible by God's love mediated through the community's love. *Sollicitudo*—that is, as we have seen, "being all in motion"—means knowing how to question ourselves, not only superficially but in depth. This solicitude excludes any kind of splitting, because it leads us to integrate positively all the dimensions of our being.

This process will certainly involve the acceptance of law. Law, understood in a broad sense as every rule that regulates and channels action, exists to serve the life of the person. The child is structured around the paternal figure, which represents the law, and we know well how indispensable this role is in making us capable of solitude, in accepting that not everything is possible, that we are not owed everything we want, and that the secret to succeed in life is the acceptance of limitations. The utter rejection of any law, norm, or limitation makes us prisoners of our own drives, disconnected from reality. Law can become an opportunity for self-mastery and therefore for growth precisely because it causes us frustrations and forces us to come to terms with them.

But *sollicitudo* must also manifest itself in the incessant and indispensable work of self-knowledge, of knowing what really motivates and inspires us, what makes us "eager"—that is, what has the power to continually put us back in motion. And if we can be motivated by the expectations of our parents or teachers, at a certain point we will also need to rely on internal motivation, on a knowledge of who we really are and what we want to do. We are all prisoners of an idealized version of ourselves, and that version is battered and scarred by life. But as it is, our authentic identity can emerge gradually, the one that is actually able to support our actions and our choices because it is based not on what others want for us but on who we really are.

Discovering our other cheek

We noted above the importance of not feeling guilty about anger, but instead listening to it and directing it positively. We recognized that feeling guilty about anger is one of the greatest obstacles to growth, not only human and psychological growth but also spiritual growth. Anger helps us grow. It is the vital and necessary force that helps us to work through challenges of all kinds. Being an instinct, a pre-rational reaction, anger is never triggered without a cause. It is neither positive nor negative; it is simply a sign that we are alive and that we want to remain so. As we said, anger never lies, so it must not be suppressed, denied, or blamed, but accepted, listened to, and honored.

In this regard, we can draw inspiration from three models of anger management offered in Scripture: Cain, Job, and Jesus.[4]

Cain was not angry at his brother Abel, he was angry at God. And the description of God's reaction is very significant: "Cain was very angry and dejected. Then the LORD said to Cain: Why are you angry? Why are you dejected? If you act rightly, you will be accepted; but if not, sin lies in wait at the door: its urge is for you, yet you can rule over it" (Gen 4:5-7). Cain's anger does not lie; it is real. It results from the feeling of having suffered injustice. Whether this is true or not, the feeling is real, and so is the pain it causes. It is a wound that needs care. And the Lord does not deny the legitimacy of this anger. On the contrary, God takes it seriously, confronts it, tries to bring it to light, wants to allow Cain to express it. In this sense, God respects and honors Cain's anger. Cain's problem is not his anger but his dejection, his rejection of the relationship. This rejection means the refusal to recognize his

4. In my comments that follow, I have drawn much inspiration from Lytta Basset, *Sainte colère: Jacob, Job, Jésus* (Paris: Bayard, 2002).

own anger, to allow himself to express it. If he had done so, he might have understood that Abel was not the cause of his anger, but only the pretext for it. He would have understood that his frustration had deeper origins and that the simple elimination of the pretext, of Abel, not only would not eliminate his dejection but would exacerbate it even more. So he holds tight to his own dejection, refuses to compare his own preconception of God with the reality of the Father who is speaking to him. He remains a prisoner of his caricature of God—that is, of an idol of his own creation—and he projects upon God his own feeling of not being valued and recognized.

Job's reaction is different from Cain's only in appearance. Facing the sudden loss of his loved ones, his social position, and finally his own health, despite his untiring loyalty to the covenant, Job does not dare to express his anger. Instead, he censors himself, destroys himself, curses himself: "After this, Job opened his mouth and cursed his day. Job spoke out and said: Perish the day on which I was born, the night when they said, 'The child is a boy!'" (Job 3:1-3). While Cain's anger unleashes its violence by destroying the other, Job twists his anger against himself, also making himself a prisoner of his own distorted vision of God, whom he perceives as a sadist . Both reactions fail to go to the root of anger, because they reject its legitimacy, ignoring it or trying to stifle it. But in doing so, they destroy the only possibility of managing it—that is, through dialogue and relationship.

This is the approach suggested by Jesus when he invites us to turn the other cheek: "When someone strikes you on [your] right cheek, turn the other one to him as well" (Matt 5:39). In other words, do not to enter into a spiral of violence in which we both destroy ourselves, but remain in relationship, look for another way. To do this, it is necessary to discover that you have "another cheek," that is, *another way of reacting*, different from the one that is suggested by your instinct or frustration. This means distancing ourselves from the evil suffered and from the distorted images of God or of others that condition us. We needn't surrender, but neither should we renounce either the relationship or the reaction. We must try to positively orient the reaction to save the relationship. We defend our perception of truth, but we also listen to that of the other. Violence erupts when conversation stops.

Winning over others

In this process of maturation, integration, and unification, we are brought back finally to the role of the formator.

We can begin by restating what we suggested above about the difference between the formator and the therapist. Experience has shown that confusing or combining the two roles is counterproductive. Therapists themselves are well aware that their role is not that of formator. The therapist listens but should not push the person. The formator, on the other hand, must encourage the person to grow up.

More precisely, our relationship with a therapist is based on transference: we project our relationship with our father or mother and whatever unresolved conflicts that may entail onto the therapist. The therapist uses this transference to help us to relive unresolved conflicts and interpret them in a new and liberating way. But this requires a rigorous management of the context: a precise hourly delimitation, the exclusion of any other interaction beyond the clinical one, and a payment for services that reminds both that this is always a simulation. Of course, even in the relationship between novices and their formator, transference is not absent. But in this context, it must be constantly defused by opening the relationship to a "third" party, represented by the community, by the form of life to be embraced, and in a certain sense also by God. The authentic formator pushes the person to grow, to achieve autonomy.

The therapist knows how to manage transference and projection and is in any case protected by the demarcation of the context—she or he can allow transference to happen precisely because the relationship is rigidly delimited. But in the case of the formator, precisely because one invests fully in the relationship and lives with the young person in the same community, it is necessary to constantly defuse every form of attachment, set limits, open the relationship, avoid the establishment of a dependence that would then become suffocating and impossible to manage.

There have been many abuses in this area, especially in recent decades. So much distrust of the use of psychology in formation is the result of the confusion between the areas of formation and psychological support, while they are in fact effective only when they are kept strictly separate, most importantly by being carried out by two different people in the two roles. This confusion between psychology and spirituality opens people to manipulation, dependency, and, often unconsciously, exploitation. This is quite the opposite of a healthy formation process in which the main objective is to promote an authentic freedom based on a healthy growth in self-knowledge and progressively lead the novices to become the main agents in managing their own affectivity and spiritual life.

"For freedom Christ set us free; so stand firm and do not submit again to the yoke of slavery" (Gal 5:1), says Paul in his letter to the Galatians. This freedom understood as the ability to choose what is good and to channel all of oneself—heart, mind, passions, and instincts—into this choice is dear to Benedict and represents the fulcrum of his formative project. The way Benedict expresses this freedom is to invite the formators not to rely on authority, even less on any form of coercion, but to know how to "win over" the novice: they must be capable, says Benedict, of "winning souls" (RB 58.6). Admittedly, to speak about "souls" is a bit obsolete. A more authentically biblical anthropology considers the person in his or her entirety, and so it is necessary to speak of winning over the whole person. A brief look at the two New Testament passages to which this sentence of Benedict refers will help us better understand its meaning.

"Winning over all" is the way Paul expresses—with almost hammering insistence—the main method of his ministry of evangelization:

> Although I am free in regard to all, I have made myself a
> slave to all so as to *win over* as many as possible. To the Jews
> I became like a Jew to *win over* Jews; to those under the law
> I became like one under the law—though I myself am not
> under the law—to *win over* those under the law. To those
> outside the law I became like one outside the law—though
> I am not outside God's law but within the law of Christ—to
> *win over* those outside the law. To the weak I became weak,
> to *win over* the weak. I have become all things to all, to save
> at least some. All this I do for the sake of the gospel, so that
> I too may have a share in it. (1 Cor 9:19-23, emphasis added)

For Paul, people are "won over" through our compassion: we
are willing to bear the burdens of the other, we seek to reach the
other from within, we situate ourselves at their own level or, rather,
we acknowledge that we are at their level. "To be weak with the
weak" is not, for Paul, humility but an awareness of his own truth,
the fruit of self-knowledge that he demonstrates when he glories
precisely in his weakness.[5]

But in the Gospel, winning over others is also the secret of the
life of an authentically Christian community: "If your brother
sins against you, go and tell him his fault between you and him
alone. If he listens to you, you have won over your brother" (Matt
18:15). The context of this passage is that of fraternal correction. It
comes immediately after the parable of the lost sheep that invites
loving and patient care for each person, not just waiting for them
to come, but going to seek them out in the most out-of-the-way
places they have ventured or hidden.

In the light of these two New Testament passages, above all
that of the lost sheep, we better understand Benedict's words in
the chapter on formation, where he states that the formator should
"*super eos omnino curiose intendat*"—"look after them [novices] with
careful attention" (RB 58.6). The Latin word *curiose* comes from

---

5. The passages abound: Rom 8:26; 2 Cor 11:30 and 12:9.

cura, in the sense expressed by the splendid image of the shepherd who tends for his sheep and above all the one who needs him most.

According to this, what wins people over is this way of taking care that reaches the other from within. This "careful attention" to the young persons in formation must take concrete form in actively helping them know their own value, a necessary precondition for their growth. In fact, only those who feel valued and recognized become able to question themselves, to actively enter into that process of self-knowledge on which their present and future spiritual, human, and emotional well-being depends.

CHAPTER IV

Leadership

[The Rule asks:] how does authority operate to set us free from fear of each other, of our own weaknesses and limitations, of our inability to satisfy what we fantasize to be the demands of a distant God?

Rowan Williams[1]

We can never pay enough attention to the topic of governance in the church, both in the case of those who have received the sacrament of orders (especially bishops, including the pope, and priests) and those with the charism of guiding a religious or monastic community (the superior or, in Benedictine monasteries, the abbot or abbess).

The New Testament is clear on this. Though it does not provide a clear image of the hierarchical structure we find in the Catholic Church today, it does foresee the roles of elders ("presbyters," cf. 1 Tim 4:14; 5:17; Titus 1:5; Jas 5:14) and "overseers" ("bishops," cf. Phil 1:1), and it repeatedly calls the baptized to loyal obedience to them. The letter to the Hebrews offers a significant example, among many others we could cite, when it states, "Obey your leaders and defer to them, for they keep watch over you and will have to give an account, that they may fulfill their task with joy

---

1. Williams, *The Way of St Benedict*, 81.

and not with sorrow, for that would be of no advantage to you" (Heb 13:17). Jesus called his apostles, who, in turn, entrusted their successors with the role of guiding the communities they founded by establishing what the Catholic Church calls "apostolic succession" and by virtue of which there are persons in charge of leading, teaching, and celebrating (the so-called *tria munera*).[2] Among the charisms or gifts that the Holy Spirit dispenses for the building up of the community (1 Cor 14:12; Eph 4:12) are those of leading (1 Cor 12:28, cf. Rom 12:6-8), shepherding, and instructing the church (Eph 4:11).

This data, however, must always be understood against the background of what constitutes Christian identity. Christianity is summed up entirely in the gift of the Holy Spirit that makes every baptized person a son or daughter in the Son and that allows her or him to call God "Father." By virtue of baptism, then, all Christians have equal dignity (cf. LG 32). The apostolic form of the church and all the charisms are entirely instrumental to the mission, to the sending (*apostle* means "sent"), to evangelization. And they are provisional—because we know that in our eternal life in God there will be "neither Jew nor Greek . . . neither slave nor free person . . . not male and female; for you are all one in Christ Jesus" (Gal 3:28), so we can say there will no longer be ordained ministries, superiors, abbots, or leaders of any kind.

This eschatological perspective has an impact on the life of the church in the present. Already an active reality, eschatology relativizes the role of leadership in the church, be it hierarchical (ordained ministry) or charismatic (superiors of religious communities, leaders of Christian communities). While certainly necessary in this phase of salvation history, the role of leading or guiding is entirely subordinated to the action of God through his Spirit and must always tend to favor, recognize, and promote this active presence of God in the community and among all the baptized.

---

2. Cf. Second Vatican Council, Dogmatic Constitution on the Church *Lumen Gentium* (henceforth, LG) 25–27.

The teaching, governing, and sanctifying roles in the church are exercised particularly (but not exclusively) by some people called and authorized for this, but these actions are authentic and effective only if they result from the action of the Spirit of Christ in the hearts. The Spirit alone sanctifies, guides, and teaches. If this does not happen, the action of ministers in the church remains vain and ineffective. The teaching of the New Testament in this regard is very clear: "The Spirit of truth, he will guide you to all truth" (John 16:13) and "the anointing that you received from [the Holy Spirit] remains in you, so that you do not need anyone to teach you" (1 John 2:27)—nor, we can add, anyone to guide you or lead you.

A quick summary of this theological principle was necessary as a basis for our reflection on the characteristics of an authentically Christian leadership. We won't try to present an elaborate theological and theoretical discourse here, but to address the question in a very practical way, using an extraordinary example whose echo was immense in the recent history of the church.

"It shall not be so among you"

I refer to the martyrdom of the seven monks of the Cistercian community of Tibhirine in Algeria in 1996, which happened in the context of the rise of Islamic fundamentalism, the brutal murder of foreigners, and the persecution of Christians and those in the local population who maintained friendly relations with them.[3] It was a dramatic episode in which the simple and obscure life of a handful of monks in a small rural village in North Africa shone so luminously that it brought light to the whole planet. In the recent history of the church, it is difficult to find a more eloquent example of the mysterious but incredible strength to

---

3. Cf. Thomas Georgeon, "Donner sa vie pour la gloire de t'aimer," *Collectanea Cisterciensia* 68 (2006): 76–104; Georgeon, "La transparence de l'absolu," *Collectanea Cisterciensia* 69 (2007): 202–225.

which Christians have access in the midst of the most desperate weaknesses, temptations, and doubts; it would be difficult to find in recent history a brighter lesson of authentically Christian leadership and vision. The vicissitudes of this community were a clear illustration of Jesus' "it shall not be so among you": "Jesus summoned them and said to them, 'You know that those who are recognized as rulers over the Gentiles lord it over them, and their great ones make their authority over them felt. But it shall not be so among you. Rather, whoever wishes to be great among you will be your servant'" (Mark 10:42-43).

A popular 2010 film, *Of Gods and Men*, by French director Xavier Beauvois, recounts in a meditative and subdued tone the harmonious relationship between these nine Trappist monks and the largely Muslim population of a small Algerian village, until seven of them were kidnapped and, a few weeks later, murdered on May 21, 1996. The film opens with a quotation from the book of Psalms: "I have said, Ye are gods; and all of you are children of the most High. But ye shall die like men, and fall like one of the princes" (Ps 82:6-7, King James Version). In fact, the film shows just the opposite—these monks did not die like the powerful of this world, but made a gift of their lives like gods or, more accurately, like God, like Christ. In fact, they did not embody leadership as this world understands it, but that of Jesus. They lived, to its most extreme consequences, Jesus' "it shall not be so among you."

The portrait of community life presented by the film is surprisingly accurate. It does not idealize the monks in any way; they are depicted in all their humanity. Most of them are not remarkable personalities, and taken individually they don't have anything special. They lead a lifestyle like that of the peasants of the neighboring village—they work in the fields, sell their products to earn a living, their common prayer is very simple, no great ceremony, no aestheticism. At times they could almost look like bachelors who lead a lifestyle that could be considered not so much austere as simply healthy and peaceful.

However, two aspects of this community immediately strike the watchful eye. The first is how different the monks are from one another in age, culture, character, and skills: an intellectual, a plumber, a doctor, a farmer, a simpleton. The only thing that unites them is their choice of monastic life. They are so different from each other that, if they had not become monks, their paths would almost certainly never have crossed. The second aspect is their exceptional proximity to the people living in the neighboring village, all Muslim. The ethnic, national, social, and cultural barriers are enormous, but something in the lifestyle of the monks, in their way of relating to others, allows their total integration into the local community. They are not considered foreigners but part of the village, to the point that this very solidarity with the surrounding population becomes one of the reasons that convinces the monks to remain despite the danger. One of the monks of the community even provided medical care for all those who turned to him. The overcoming of these normally impassable cultural, ethnic, and religious barriers testifies to the authenticity of these monks. Such a miracle is possible only if there is a true humanity. The monks speak a universal language—the language of work, of hospitality, of common prayer, a language that people of every culture and every religion understand, including those who do not believe. The secret of an authentic monastic spirituality is precisely this: the Gospel is transmitted not primarily through words, but in the most fundamental gestures and activities of work, care for creation, and ways of relating to others.

This miracle of peaceful coexistence was brutally disrupted with the start of the civil war in Algeria in the mid-1990s, which involved a corrupt government supported by a particularly ferocious army as well as groups of Islamic terrorists who targeted foreigners within the nation's borders. After a series of brutal murders, all foreigners—including the monks of Tibhirine—were invited to leave Algeria. The monks, in fact, were particularly exposed to these threats, since everyone knew where they were, they had no defense, and their killing would have an enormous symbolic significance.

The results of this fatal alchemy are tragically well known.

When the prior of the community, Christian de Chergé, refuses the protection of the corrupt civil authorities, the monks are divided among themselves about whether to stay in Algeria or leave the country. Before this decision is made, a group of Islamic terrorists, led by Ali Fayattia, bursts into the monastery on Christmas Eve to kidnap the medical brother and commandeer the scarce medical supplies that the monks kept available for the poor. The prior refuses to comply with these demands that would have hurt the poor by quoting the Qur'an. And, surprisingly, Fayattia agrees to leave empty-handed and grants his protection to the community until he himself is captured, tortured, and killed by government forces.

Despite the growing danger, the monks choose solidarity with the local population over fleeing, even at the risk of their lives. Then one night another group of armed terrorists kidnaps them and holds them hostage for several weeks. The last scene of the film shows the line of captive monks, escorted by their captors, trudging along a snowy path and disappearing into the fog, while in the background you hear the voice of the prior reading his spiritual testament.

Vision and strength

The link between this story and the topic of leadership is that it presents an exceptional lesson of authentically Christian leadership and offers rich food for thought regarding the dynamics of community discernment.

It is not difficult to recognize what a visionary the prior of the community, Christian de Chergé, was: he believed unconditionally in the possibility of true solidarity between men and women of all races and religions; he openly acknowledged in his will that his violent death at the hands of Islamic extremists would confirm the opinion of those who considered him naive or idealistic; he learned Arabic, read the Qur'an. He was a man of absolute integrity, of deep prayer. In reference to leadership, Christian certainly had the fundamental characteristics of a true leader: vision and strength. And the people around him recognized it. The brothers of his community respected him; these qualities even elicited the respect of the leader of the group of Islamic terrorists, Ali Fayattia. To resist the threats of terror and the bullying of both the terrorists and the army required an uncommon strength. Christian could do it because he had a very clear vision of the vocation of the community: Jesus would not have wanted armed protection, he would have remained despite the danger, and he would not have abandoned the people of the village who were threatened both by the terrorists and by the army just as much as the monks were.

But for an authentically Christian leadership, vision and strength are not enough. They are indispensable for a leader, but in certain circumstances they can blind him, as happened in the Tibhirine community in the situation we are recalling.

We are shown a community meeting, a normal event in the life of a monastic community. According to the Rule of Benedict, every time there is an important decision to be made, the abbot must summon the monks, explain the situation and open it for discussion, then listen carefully to their opinions and only then make a decision (RB 3). The rule emphasizes the importance of humility and moderation with which the monks should express their views, as well as the need for the superior to proceed with prudence and equity (RB 3.6) and to do nothing without first seeking advice (RB 3.13).

At this community meeting, a tension immediately surfaces. Without realizing it, the prior has not gathered the community to seek its advice, but to inform it of a decision that he has already made—that is, to remain despite great risks. Several of the brothers are irritated that he has made a decision that involves their own safety, taking their consent for granted and failing to respect their feelings, their fears, and their need to choose such a risk freely. It is important to understand that the brothers do not dispute their superior's good intentions, nor the wisdom of his decision. Even the most irritated already know, after all, that this is the only way forward. But this awareness is not enough.

The more a leader has the qualities of vision and strength, the more he is likely to find himself in situations like this. A true leader constantly reflects to determine the best direction to follow. He or she must draw upon considerable internal motivation and energy to be able to deal with external and internal pressures and have the courage to make decisions that he knows to be the right ones, even if they are often not understood or accepted by everyone else. He or she needs this vision and this strength above all to face his own doubts, hesitations, and fears. Every big decision is accompanied by anxiety, sometimes by anguish. A leader needs to be able to trust something deeper than reasons, to resort to a kind of instinct, and for this he must be in contact with a deep part of himself, without ever yielding to irrationality. The dilemma for a leader, however, is that the very vision and strength that are necessary to govern with foresight can sometimes lead him to lose contact with reality. Vision and strength are not enough to guarantee that a decision is authentically Christian. Something more is needed.

Heroes and martyrs

To widen the perspective, let's pause in our reflection and focus for a moment on one aspect of the story of this monastic community. During the resurgence of Islamic extremism in Algeria during those years, nineteen Christians, including an exceptional bishop, were murdered. But only the martyrdom of the seven monks of Tibhirine has produced a worldwide echo, striking the collective imagination and burning itself into the memory of millions of people. Just like the monks of Tibhirine, the other twelve Christian martyrs died because of their faith. Why did the martyrdom of these monks generate such a distinctive echo?

Add to this that the details of their deaths are marked by some uncertainty. From the beginning, the film warns of how much they risk becoming a pawn in a game bigger than themselves and that their deaths would leave a taste of manipulation. Even today it has not been determined precisely how they perished and at the hands of whom—Islamic terrorists or the army? It is not yet known whether their killing was intentional or accidental. The most likely case is that it happened by mistake. Nobody really wanted to kill them. It seems that the Islamic terrorists only wanted to take them captive in order to use them for an exchange of prisoners, but during an attack by the army against the Islamists, the monks were killed, and then attempts were made to throw off the investigations, so that only their decapitated heads were eventually found.

It is a story in which good and evil are ambiguous, and the film depicts this eloquently—the Islamists recognize the men of God; the army says it wants to protect people but ends up eliminating the witnesses of its abuses; in the end the same fog swallows both the monks and their captors.

One might say that what made them martyrs was not their decision to remain despite the danger, nor even their deaths. All that we know of the lives of these monks, especially during the months that preceded their abduction, demonstrates that they were not what many would consider heroes or that perhaps only some of them could have been considered as such. But heroism in such circumstances can be ambiguous; it can become a form of self-affirmation at the expense of others. This is especially the temptation of every leader—doing great things, acquiring a reputation, gaining admiration for things imposed on others. We need to be open to other criteria to measure success in leadership. Such success must take into account factors beyond results. The background of the story of the Tibhirine community is very instructive in this regard.

Conflict

Let us return to the community meeting mentioned above. Several monks are still shocked by the recent nighttime terrorist incursion. The prior, while not ignoring these fears and tensions, has already made the decision to remain despite the danger and to refuse the protection of the army. He takes the consensus of the community on this point for granted. He has confidence in his vision and is aware of his strength. He knows that he can impose his decision based not so much on the authority of his office as by playing the moral obligation card. He is strong in his moral integrity, in his intellectual and, above all, spiritual superiority. He has taken the time to let this decision mature within himself, through deep reflection and long hours of prayer. He knows that his duty now is to set an example of courage and firmness.

The dynamics of the meeting show how healthy the community is. The brothers respect and love their superior, they admire him, and they do not question his motivations. But they feel free to express their disagreement and their fears. They are not afraid of conflict; on the contrary, they have learned that it must be addressed, and they know they can face it responsibly together. They know they need to help their superior hear and take into consideration their hesitation, their fears, and, above all, their right to participate actively in a decision that concerns their survival.

In this moment of truth, the prior is caught off guard, and we see him living one of the painful experiences typical of every leader's life. Aware of how much his decision is demanding of himself, he is tempted to feel misunderstood. He is tempted to consider the community's reaction as ingratitude and consequently to fall back on himself and play the moral superiority card. In fact, he tries to barricade himself behind the vision: "We are men of peace. We cannot arm ourselves or have ourselves protected by the weapons of others. Monks must be unarmed." But the brothers answer him, "You are not listening to us." Christian does not want to accept the hesitations and weaknesses of his brothers, and perhaps he cannot afford it. He fears that exposing himself to the weaknesses and hesitations of his confreres also involves acknowledging his own, which he has prematurely put aside.

At that moment, he becomes aware that there are other ways of being armed. He understands that he is armed against his brothers and that they are armed against him, because they are afraid of not being heard and they need to defend themselves. The confreres who want to stay are armed, because they feel they're on the side of reason, but unconsciously they fear taking into consideration the weakness and fear of others and above all to have to recognize the legitimacy of that fear. The confreres who want to leave are armed, not because they do not want to give their lives to the Lord, but because they do not feel involved in this decision, they have not had time to accept it internally, they have not been heard.

A shared decision

The role of the prior in this situation is decisive. These moments are a test of the spiritual and human depth of a leader. Exposed to the temptation to consider such opposition as a refusal of his leadership, a personal rebuke, the prior doesn't yield to the instinct of self-defense and closure on himself, but discovers himself mysteriously able to open up, to expose himself. He recognizes in this humiliation a call to a deeper conversion, to a new "birth" as he himself will later say. He recognizes that it is necessary to allow the time to transform a *right* decision into a *shared* decision, to move from an imposed decision to a consensus that not only takes everyone into account but involves their humanity—their intelligence and will, but also their desires, fears, feelings, and passions.

The vision itself then expands. It is not enough to say that the monks *must* be disarmed against terrorists; they are called first of all to commit themselves to being disarmed against each other. There are many ways to take up arms, and one of the most fatal is precisely the refusal to listen to each other, the refusal to take into account the weaknesses and fears of others because they awaken our own that we would prefer to ignore.

Compassion

This is the most painful but also the most fruitful moment of conversion in the life of a leader. This is the moment in which Jesus' admonition comes true: "But it shall not be so among you" (Mark 10:43). "Do not be like the leaders of this world." Vision and strength for a leader are indispensable, but a leader can exercise authentically Christian leadership only when open to *compassion*.

It is of paramount importance that during this decisive meeting the prior allows himself to be questioned and then even takes sides with those who are not ready to make a decision, accepting the need to wait, courageously embracing the process necessary to integrate the fears, weaknesses, and hesitations of others and his own.

Unknowingly, both the prior and the community undergo a fundamental discernment at this juncture, that which turns their decision to remain despite the danger into authentic martyrdom. As the prior will later recognize, at that moment they realized that it was they themselves who had to lay down their arms, to allow themselves to be disarmed. They become martyrs because they allow themselves to be disarmed. And the extraordinary eloquence of their martyrdom derives from having made this decision together, in conformity with the great principle of Benedictine asceticism, the keystone of the spirituality of the Rule: the *omnes pariter*, the "all together" that concludes Chapter 72.

Particularly in accordance with Benedictine spirituality is that this process of maturation has unfolded through the peaceful *ora et labora*, through simple rites and gestures of everyday life. As Christian would later say, "We had to go on living. . . . Our salvation was to have to take up the daily reality: the kitchen, the garden, the office, the bell." The decision to remain, a decision that involves the whole community and fully integrates the humanity of each of the monks, matures through the rhythm of fraternal life: the moments of silent prayer, the walks, singing together, celebrating the Eucharist together, friendship between them and with neighbors.

The monks understood that it was necessary to give the extraordinary strength of their fraternity the time to deploy its potential. In the course of this gestation, the "heroes" allowed themselves to be disarmed of their pride, the weak learned to overcome their fear, and both supported each other in preparing for a gift of self that was consensual, mature, and as free from presumption as it was from hesitation.

In this we have an authentic, paradigmatic representation of Christian holiness. Fragile, hesitant people, tempted by pride and weakness like any other human being, are granted the access to an authentically evangelical witness—that is, "martyrdom"—thanks to the strength of community life. They understand that if their mission is to be brothers of all, even to their enemies, it is because they live this brotherhood with each other and with their neighbors every day. They do not even judge the terrorists, because community life helps them daily to become aware of their complicity with the evil of the world.

It will always be possible to challenge monastic spirituality for the decision to take a certain distance from the world and to draw attention to the danger that this attitude may become an escape from one's duty to contribute to building a more just and more humane society. But the extraordinary echo of the testimony of the monks of Tibhirine shows that there are different ways of playing this role, of contributing to this building up of society, and of proclaiming the Gospel. These monks testify to the importance of taking, at times, a certain distance from the world in order to enter into a deeper relationship with it. They demonstrate that one can be a missionary by going to the people, but also by creating spaces of fraternity where everyone, of any creed or condition of life, can feel welcomed, loved, helped, and heard.

Finally, this testimony illustrates the conversion process necessary to access a genuinely evangelical style of leadership. Only compassion allows the vision and strength of a leader to be tools not only of personal affirmation but of growth of the community entrusted to him. And there is no compassion without conversion and without lengthy processes of gestation in which it can seem that a leader is being slowed down, when in reality he is simply letting his vision acquire the human depth that will ensure truly lasting results.

CHAPTER V

Forgiving

*It was a mechanism within which the participants
had got themselves caught up in such a way that they
couldn't perceive what they were doing. The moment I
realised that I was dealing with a mechanism whose
participants were its prisoners, at that same moment
I was able to take distance from what had happened,
and forgiveness started to become possible.*

James Alison[1]

There is no area of Christian life where we experience our
powerlessness more profoundly than in the call to forgive. It is
impossible to hear what the Gospel teaches about forgiveness
without being seized by a sense of discouragement. How often
we try to forgive, not to react to evil, not to give in to resentment,
but fail. Or how many times we manage to overcome animosity
or negative thoughts for a while, only to feel our hearts harden
again later and bitterness take over. Sometimes we manage to
forgive outwardly, but in our hearts we cannot avoid feeling hatred
for the people who hurt us, and so we avoid them or speak badly
about them. We continue to be cold, distant, indifferent, or, worse,

---

1. James Alison, *Faith Beyond Resentment: Fragments Catholic and Gay* (New
York: Crossroad, 2001), 38.

we discover that we cannot resist rejoicing when those who have harmed us suffer. When something unpleasant happens to them, we are tempted to see it as a just punishment.

Recognizing this fact is fundamental: forgiving truly, forgiving evangelically, is not easy.

Neither hyperbole nor rule

There are two possible reactions to the radical nature of Jesus' teaching on forgiveness. The first is to consider it hyperbole, a rhetorical exaggeration: Jesus does not *really* expect us to turn the other cheek or to give away our shirt along with our coat (cf. Luke 6:29). An exaggeration like this would be typical of the Semitic language, as when Jesus says, "If your right eye causes you to sin, tear it out and throw it away" (Matt 5:29; 18:9). The other reaction is to consider the teaching on forgiveness a simple moral rule: Jesus says that I must forgive my enemies and love them, so I just have to do it. If I haven't succeeded so far, if I couldn't forgive, it's because I haven't tried hard enough or haven't really wanted to. Both these ways of understanding the Gospel are wrong.

First, we know that these words of the Gospel are not an exaggeration for a very simple reason: Jesus' own example. Jesus never tore out an eye, nor did he ever ask anyone else to—that one really is a rhetorical exaggeration. But in the case of forgiveness, Jesus really did not resist those who arrested, tortured, and murdered him. He continued to love Judas and washed his feet during the Last Supper, gave his life for him, presented his cheek for the kiss of betrayal, did not react, continued to offer his face to those who slapped it. He gave no answer to those who dragged him to court, did not defend himself, knowing that they were not looking for the truth and that it was useless to speak. On the cross he prayed for those who were killing him and sought for them the Father's forgiveness: "Father, forgive them, they know not what they do" (Luke 23:34). So Jesus' teaching about forgiveness is no rhetorical exaggeration. His own example makes clear that he means it literally.

But just as mistaken would be a purely moralistic interpretation that would make forgiveness simply a question of following a rule, a choice we make. This interpretation is wrong because it is impossible to forgive. The best we're able to do is to pretend to forget about what has hurt us. But that is not really forgiveness, because hostility, anger, and resentment remain under a false facade, and if we peel away some of the new paint, the old grudges and resentments are still there, just as real and just as strong. Jesus' teaching about forgiveness is much more than just a moral rule.

Meeting the Father's eyes

If we truly reflect on this teaching, we will come to understand that forgiveness is possible only thanks to a context that we have to create slowly, patiently, diligently. And this context has two main characteristics. First, our hearts become capable of forgiving only if, rather than closing ourselves up in ourselves, we raise our eyes to meet the eyes of our Father who is in heaven. Second, forgiveness develops and thrives only in the context of a community of solidarity and only if we consider it to be a shared responsibility. Let's examine these two aspects more closely.

In the first place, the failure to forgive is a result of self-isolation. This is particularly evident in the story, which we have already encountered, of the first murder, that of Cain killing Abel. We read in the book of Genesis that because the Lord did not look with favor on Cain's offering, "Cain was very angry and dejected. Then the LORD said to Cain: Why are you angry? Why are you dejected? If you act rightly, you will be accepted; but if not, sin lies in wait at the door: its urge is for you, yet you can rule over it" (Gen 4:6-7). The Hebrew word that is translated here as *dejected* literally means "his face was turned down." The hatred, the resentment, the desire for revenge are manifested through a downturned face, a look that avoids that of God, a refusal to meet God's eyes. If we listen to the monologue of resentment, bitterness, hatred, and desire for revenge that occupies our minds sometimes for entire days, we will always find ourselves muttering things like "I can't let anyone do this to me," "I refuse to be treated like this," "I must defend my reputation," and so on. The truth is that bitterness, animosity, resentment, and the desire for revenge are not natural feelings for us. These negative feelings are foreign to our hearts and our spirits—they can grow and end up determining our behavior only if we nurture them, only if we constantly blow on them like the embers of a fire that we want to keep burning.

This is why Scripture says, "Take no revenge and cherish no grudge against your own people" (Lev 19:18). The dynamic of revenge requires a cold and blind deliberation nurtured over time. It requires perseverance in evil. I begin by closing myself in upon myself; then I keep telling myself that I cannot afford to be humiliated in this way; then I let the initial pain and resentment, which were basically manageable, grow and evolve into open hostility; then I fall prey to bitterness, then to frustration, and finally to a hate that is thirsty for satisfaction and revenge.

We mustn't try to justify animosity, resentment, or revenge by attributing them to our survival instinct, as if they were simply methods of self-defense. Of course, when we feel our lives are in danger, we defend ourselves. In extreme situations, self-defense can justify the physical disabling of those who want to hurt us. This legitimizes the exercise of retributive justice in society. But for it to be an authentic form of *justice*, it must never be motivated by resentment, hatred, or, worse, the desire for revenge. To remain just, it must be objective; it must simply protect, repair the wrong, and strive to rehabilitate those who have done evil. Jesus himself acted in this way—he warned us against sin, but he wants us not to abandon the sinner. Or rather, he warned us against sin in order to lead sinners to repentance. Resentment and bitterness, not to mention hatred and revenge, can never pretend to be forms of the instinct for self-preservation or self-defense. They can never be considered expressions of justice.

On the contrary, they are forms of a pride well illustrated by Lamech's chilling threat in the fourth chapter of the book of Genesis: "I have killed a man for wounding me, / a young man for bruising me. / If Cain is avenged seven times, / then Lamech seventy-seven times" (Gen 4:23-24). What worse form of pride is there than boasting of hatred, reducing the other persons to the evil they have done to me, refusing to acknowledge that fault and responsibility are almost never one-sided? The dynamics of resentment and bitterness that lead to hatred are forms of insanity. They "corrode" us inside, imprison us in paranoia. It is no coincidence that we speak of "blinding hatred." Hence the impossibility of truly forgiving without first having been cured of our blindness, helped to overcome our self-isolation, and freed from our pride.

This is why we are not able to offer real forgiveness with a simple act of will, but only through a patient and sometimes long *process*. Scripture teaches us a lot in this regard—for example, in the way God treats Cain. God does not confront Cain by immediately ordering him to forgive Abel. First, he invites Cain to re-establish the dialogue with the Father, with the Lord, to turn to him: "Why are you angry? Why are you dejected [literally: why is your face turned down]?" (Gen 4:6). We could interpret this as an invitation to pray, parallel to that of Jesus' "Pray for those who persecute you" (Matt 5:44). God invites Cain, as Jesus invites each of us, to look upward: "Don't look at the ground—lift your eyes, look me in the eyes!" In the Gospel of Matthew, the process of forgiveness begins by looking to the Father who "makes his sun rise on the bad and the good, and causes rain to fall on the just and the unjust" (Matt 5:45). Only the Lord, the Father, "pardons all your sins, / and heals all your ills" (Ps 103:3), as the psalm says, and of what more serious illness do we need to be healed than the pride, resentment, and animosity that grips our hearts?

Anyone who has received the grace of authentic forgiveness knows that it is like a knot that is suddenly untied, a rock removed from our heart. It is not by chance that liberation from bitterness and resentment is often accompanied by tears—not tears of pain, but of liberation and joy. The first phase in the process of forgiveness, then, is to be torn from closure upon ourselves, from isolation, from separation from God and from others.

A shared endeavor

There is a second decisive phase in this process, which the Gospel suggests through a detail that is easily missed, especially in English. When Jesus speaks of the process of forgiveness, he alternates between the second-person singular ("you" addressed to one person) and second-person plural ("you" addressed to more than one person, to a group). When he says, "I say to you, offer no resistance to one who is evil. When someone strikes you on your right cheek, turn the other one to him as well. If anyone wants to go to law with you over your tunic, hand him your cloak as well. Should anyone press you into service for one mile, go with him for two miles" (Matt 5:39-41), in each case, he speaks in the second-person singular. But then in the following sentences, he speaks in the second-person plural when he says, "I say to you, love your enemies, and pray for those who persecute you. . . . Be perfect, just as your heavenly Father is perfect" (Matt 5:44, 48). This suggests that forgiveness is possible only within a community, only with the help and support of a community. Forgiveness depends not only or even principally on an isolated "I" but also on a "we." It is something that can blossom and grow only within a community where love and forgiveness are cultivated.

This confirms what we said above: resentment, revenge, and hatred are always expressions of the rejection of our solidarity with others—I no longer want to consider others my sisters or brothers; it is easier to reduce them to whatever evil they did to me. Let's reflect on this: is it not odd that a person for whom I feel only dislike and animosity should be respected and loved by other people? This is the result of the blindness caused by hostility—I see my sister or brother only as a threat to me. Hatred, resentment, and revenge thrive in a society of competing individuals. This is why the most frequent areas of conflict are sexuality and work, where competition dominates, where the advantage of one is too often understood to come at the expense of another.

But forgiveness flourishes in a community of brothers and sisters who strive to live in solidarity and shared responsibility, in which relationships are not guided by sexual instinct or competition, but where the good of the other also becomes my good, where I can find joy in the well-being and success of others. Forgiveness can flourish only where there is dialogue and mutual help.

It is inevitable that in every community, every family, and every professional relationship, misunderstandings, hostilities, jealousies, and passions arise. But thanks be to God, they do not affect everyone at the same time and with the same intensity. They are not normally all oriented toward the same people, and they do not arise in everyone for the same reasons. Thus it is possible to help each other forgive.

This is the context in which to practice the wonderful beatitude, "Blessed are the peacemakers, for they will be called children of God" (Matt 5:9), which could be rephrased as "Blessed are the facilitators of forgiveness." We are all called to be peacemakers in this way. We must all strive to promote forgiveness so that as soon as we detect seeds of misunderstanding or jealousy, or we perceive grudges or resentments, we avoid throwing fuel on the fire through gossip or siding with one or the other. On the contrary, with discretion and patience—and without being condescendent either—we must all commit ourselves to healing wounds, reconciling enemies, correcting those who seem to be wrong, mediating conflicts.

It is no coincidence that there is such a close relationship between the beatitude on peacemaking and Jesus' teaching on forgiveness. After all, he teaches that peacemakers are blessed because "they will be called children of God" and, later in the same discourse, that we must love our enemies and pray for them "that you may be children of your heavenly Father." In both cases these behaviors are a privileged expression of being children of the Father.

For this reason, forgiveness is not and cannot be a mere question of will. It must be recognized as a process that requires a common strategy, imagination, intelligence, and diplomacy, and it prospers only if we feel truly in solidarity with one another, if we feel responsible for one another.

That's why we must never be discouraged when we experience our inability to forgive. The Lord has not told us that it is a simple thing or a quick process. Forgiveness must be built day after day and, paradoxically, we achieve it not by trying to force ourselves to forgive at all costs, but above all by committing ourselves to act as peacemakers, as nurturers of forgiveness in the communities of which we are a part. The more I commit myself to help others forgive, the more I can hope that when I need to forgive, I will find at my side a peacemaker who will help me.

Just as resentment, bitterness, and hatred lead to pride that isolates us, encloses us in ourselves, blinds us, so forgiveness is built on humility that helps us recognize that we need help. We need help to forgive; we can't do it alone. Forgiveness needs humility that welcomes advice and is ready to ask for it. When I have trouble forgiving, I have to know how to ask for help. I have to know how to go to someone who can help me. Forgiveness needs humility that brings peace. We need humility to pray for those who hurt us, and, above all, we need humility to continue to hope against all hope.

Forgiveness, then, is not impossible, but that doesn't mean it's as simple as just deciding to forgive. Forgiveness is something we must build, toward which we must work with patience, and that flourishes only if we live the spirit of the beatitudes as a community: "Blessed are the peacemakers, for they will be called children of God" (Matt 5:9).

CHAPTER VI

Chastity

*"Before the 60s, celibates were presumed to have
no sexuality" [said one study participant]. . . .
[E]ven priests who know "hundreds and hundreds
of priests" often do not know the sexual/celibate
adjustment of even their closest friends, as we found
time and time again in our search. This adjustment
is mostly a secret one.*

Richard Sipe[1]

If we want to understand chastity, we can begin by seeing it simply as "life." We want to live. A monk used to pray thus, "Lord, let me be still alive when I will die."

Many consider a monastic's existence to be a negation of life. Why set limits to our freedom by choosing to obey? Why turn away from the possession of material goods and the use of money? And why, above all, renounce sexual relationships? Many would say that this is not life, and they might not be entirely wrong.

---

1. Richard Sipe, *A Secret World: Sexuality and the Search for Celibacy* (New York: Brunner-Routledge, 1990), 4–5.

Life

And yet we become monastics because we want to live. "As he was setting out on a journey, a man ran up, knelt down before him, and asked him, 'Good teacher, what must I do to inherit eternal life?'" (Mark 10:17). "Eternal life" means a full life, fullness of life, fullness of meaning. The young man asks, "Master, what must I do to feel truly alive, in order to be alive when I die?" This question initiates a dialogue between the young man and Jesus:

> Jesus answered him, "Why do you call me good? No one is good but God alone. You know the commandments: 'You shall not kill; you shall not commit adultery; you shall not steal; you shall not bear false witness; you shall not defraud; honor your father and your mother.'" He replied and said to him, "Teacher, all of these I have observed from my youth." Jesus, looking at him, loved him and said to him, "You are lacking in one thing. Go, sell what you have, and give to the poor and you will have treasure in heaven; then come, follow me." At that statement his face fell, and he went away sad, for he had many possessions. (Mark 10:18-22)

Before we even open our mouths, the Lord knows us. He knows our inconsistencies, our ambitions, the weaknesses of our will. He does not yield to the young man's flattery ("good teacher"). The young man is one of those people who covers others with compliments in order to subdue them and subtly manipulate them. They want approval, not relationship. To succumb to them is to permit them to use us, to support them in their conviction of being able to obtain everything through seduction and leaving them prisoners of their cynicism. Maybe we reassure ourselves by telling ourselves that we are not the seducers. True or not, we certainly have one thing in common with the young man: we don't really know ourselves. We say things to ourselves, to others, to God, but we don't really think about them or measure their meaning. We are like Peter, who said to Jesus, "Master, why can't I follow you now? I will lay down my life for you" (John 13:37). He believes he really wants what he says, but Jesus reveals that he doesn't know himself, doesn't know his own weakness: "Will you lay down your life for me? Amen, amen, I say to you, the cock will not crow before you deny me three times" (John 13:38).

Jesus reveals to us the truth about ourselves. He shows us our dark side, the part that resists life, happiness, and the realization of ourselves. There is an idolatrous aspect in our personality, a lack of freedom, and Jesus has his own way of making us aware of it—not a pitiless unmasking, but an invitation to step out of ourselves, to dare to open our eyes to the light of day. In our interpretation of Jesus' call to the young man, let us not stop at "Go and sell," at renunciation, but let us go to the real invitation: "Come, follow me!"

Jesus does not ask the young man to *abandon something*, but to *embrace someone*. He tells him, "Follow me." That is, he calls him to choose love, to choose relationship rather than possession. And there is a bitter irony in the evangelist's comment at the end of this passage: "At that statement his face fell, and he went away sad, for he had many possessions" (Mark 10:22). Possessions are good in themselves, but when we let ourselves be possessed by them, they stifle every other desire. They cause our hearts to shrivel. Instead of giving us joy, they leave us sad, with fallen faces.

This applies not only to goods and possessions. Any gift or talent can be distorted and become a prison. Even sexuality, physical attraction, our bodies, our need to love and be loved—all of these can be corrupted in this way. They exist to connect us, to unite us with another person, to give us joy, to make us live. But they can lead us to use others as if they were things, to seek fulfillment at the expense of other people, and in giving us pleasure they leave bitterness in our mouths, they enclose us in ourselves. The young man turns his back on the offer of a relationship, and he goes away sad and alone.

But this story does not condemn us to pessimism because it is *gospel*—that is, "good news." The good news is that there is a remedy for idolatry, for this inadequate way of relating to ourselves and others, for this attitude that turns gifts and talents into a prison. The remedy is in Jesus' invitation, "Follow me." The remedy to idolatry is authentic relationship, the relationship that sets us free, the "chaste" relationship. In fact, we can define chastity as a type of relationship with myself and with others that frees love, preserves freedom, and allows me to realize myself, to live fully. Chastity is a gift. Chastity is freedom. Chastity is the free relationship.

But there is more "news" in this story that does not immediately appear as "good" (as "gospel") and that becomes a source of consolation only if it is understood correctly. This other good news is that left to ourselves, we are incapable of free and authentic relationships. Maybe we will not be slaves of possessions and goods like this young man, but we all must deal with an intrinsic egoism, a visceral fear of losing control of our lives, of not realizing ourselves, with the fear of—to use Jesus' words—"losing our life" (cf. Mark 8:35), even if it were for love, for God. This egoism and fear are inevitable, and when they take hold of us, they threaten chastity; that is, they compromise healthy relationships with ourselves, with others, and with God.

Yet right here, right in the heart of what seems to be our most humiliating limitation, our most crushing failure, right here we are met with good news. Yes, it is true, as far as it depends on us it is a lost battle, it is impossible. But "all things are possible for God" (Mark 10:27), love is stronger than death (cf. Song 8:6), and we have a promise: Neither death, nor life, nor angels, nor principalities, nor present things, nor future things, nor powers, nor height, nor depth, nor any other creature, nor our own incompetence, nor our weakness, nor the tumult of our passions, nor our unruly instincts will be able to separate us from the love of God in Christ Jesus our Lord (cf. Rom 8:38-39).

Celibate but not chaste[2]

In speaking, then, of this chastity, this relationship, this life, we must distinguish it from celibacy. It is possible, in fact, to be celibate but not chaste.

---

2. "Celibacy" here means renouncing all kind of sexual acts, while "chastity" means "loving attention to the other person" in all relationships, including sexual intercourse.

Why do monastics embrace celibacy? Why do they choose not to marry? There comes a moment of truth in life when we must admit to ourselves that we have perhaps embraced celibacy for the wrong reasons—fear of our own sexuality; nonacceptance of our body; a refuge where one hopes to sublimate or suppress a homosexual tendency; escape from relationships; and so on. In short, we may have to admit that we have not embraced celibacy in order to live, but to avoid facing a rebellious or unmanageable part of ourselves, using it in fact as a kind of armor or shield.

Celibacy according to the Gospel is exactly the opposite. It is not denial of one's body, one's impulses, or one's tendencies, but a way to take them seriously, welcome them, and honor them. Accepting one's body, impulses, and tendencies does not mean simply satisfying them, like scratching an itch. These impulses are a language; they have a profound meaning, tell us something, yearn for something. However messy or clumsy, they are expressions of our need to love and be loved, to receive and give life. In order to be understood and honored, these impulses need to be integrated into relationships that are free and faithful, relationships that give us joy and through which we can give joy to other people.

Only in this way does celibacy become chaste. And it is the same way that all other kinds of relationships—whether friendship, married life, or community life—become chaste. Chastity is the secret to healthy relationships in every lifestyle—for the priest, the monastic, married people, those who have chosen cohabitation (the majority today) and same-sex couples. In each of these life choices, relationships thrive only if they are chaste, only if the other person is not an object I possess through sex or power (and often more through power than sex), but someone I love for himself or herself.

Sexuality permeates all our relationships, because each of them involves emotions. Sexuality is the emotional aspect in each of our relationships. It is the strength, the energy generated when in contact with another person. I need other people. I can't live without other people. I cannot grow without affection given and received, without exchanges that give me joy and recognition. The relationships in which I am reduced to my function or idealized alienate me. They reduce me to the status of object.

And so chastity is a *space* in which I am respected, I become more and more the subject or agent of my own life, and I allow the other to exist for him- or herself. I love the other for him- or herself. It is the opposite of unhealthy attachment, which eliminates the distance and in which the two, both I and the other, cease to exist.

A chaste relationship is built, preserved, and consecrated through words, the right words. For our affective life we certainly need to touch and be touched, to see and be seen, but even more do we need words. Even more than touching and seeing, words unite, preserving the difference, respecting the right distance, allowing reciprocity.

Turmoil

But sexuality is also turmoil!

> I was sleeping, but my heart was awake.
>> The sound of my lover knocking!
> "Open to me, my sister, my friend,
>> my dove, my perfect one!
> For my head is wet with dew,
>> my hair, with the moisture of the night."
> . . . .
> My lover put his hand in through the opening:
>> my innermost being trembled because of him. (Song 5:2-4)

In the Song of Songs, when the beloved is in sight, his lover's insides tingle. In the same way, every so often—more often at some times, less often at others—our whole being tingles in the presence of an external stimulus. Sometimes it is a stimulus that we seek, like when we look at pornographic images. But then the turmoil is limited and soon gives way to boredom. We quiver more when the stimulus is unexpected, when it catches us off guard—a look, an advertising image, the page of a novel, a memory. Then we are unarmed and even a little humiliated. We are not sure if we are accomplices or not. We are tempted to blame ourselves and may even feel threatened.

The challenge then is not to give in to fear, but to welcome this disturbance as a gift, a blessing, a positive symptom. If I am upset, in fact, it is because I remain open and do not deny my dependence on things and people external to me and over which I have no power. *The turmoil is the antidote to thinking we're omnipotent.* The great lesson that our sexuality gives us every day is that we need other people. Who I am is, in a sense, what all my encounters with other people in my life have made me. And while I depend on those around me to live and to grow, this also makes me vulnerable to the disturbances they bring—it is normal and necessary.

Chastity is not the absence of turmoil; it is a covenant between love and turmoil. Chastity does not fear turmoil but welcomes it as a blessing, as a call to a greater integration of my personality, to a more mature awareness of my abilities and my limitations, to more courage in accepting the animal side of my personality, to learn to love the beast in me. Of course, it's true that turmoil scares us and must be taken seriously because it can lead us to sadness and alienation. But the road from turmoil to alienation is long, and there is ample space to negotiate with my sexual instinct without becoming an accomplice, without yielding to it superficially, but to grant it what it genuinely desires.

Negotiation

The secret is in *negotiation*. The sexual instinct cannot be simply controlled; it must be approached with diplomatic expertise. But to master this skill, a conversion is needed first. We must overcome the confusion between chastity and perfection. Perfection is inhuman; it is a form of omnipotence, and it comes at a cost since it cuts us off from reality. Chastity, on the other hand, is porous, open, flexible, full of imagination, and, above all, bold. Perfection can't bend, so it breaks; in fact, it always ends up in shatters. Among the most emblematic of the sex scandals in the church in recent decades was the one involving the founder of the Legionaries of Christ. In this order, absolute discipline—immaculate cassocks, perfectly starched clerical collars, flawless rituals—was the curtain that allowed decades of abuse to thrive undisturbed.

Chastity makes sense only if we renounce perfection, accept our humanity to the full, stop aspiring to live in an idealized world and accept our history, body, passions, instincts, desires, hesitations, and failures as integral and unavoidable parts of our identity.

It is certainly legitimate to have an ideal and to try to guide our impulses, passions, and sexuality according to it. But ideal and sexuality can only join forces by avoiding slipping into the blind alley of an idealized vision of chastity that would claim abstract, static control of living matter, of the energy of which we are made, in the logic of all or nothing. In this dynamic I am either chaste or not, and if I am not, then I must become chaste simply by deciding to.

A story

Instead, each of us is a story. The ideal is not some kind of armor that we wear to restrain and protect ourselves. The ideal is a breath, an impulse, a spirit that flows from within, from the depths of ourselves. It grows, and this growth requires time and patience. The idealized image of chastity is impersonal and abstract; it makes everything depend on reason and will. In Christian logic, on the other hand, chastity is an invitation: "Follow me!" It means entering a covenant, a story. It is relationship; it is allowing the Lord, others, and ourselves to love each other as we are, where we are. It means silencing guilt. If we are an ongoing story, then where we are now is not as important as where we are going and where we want to go, or rather where we are being led, accompanied, and awaited. We must always resist the temptation to see only where we are now, frozen in place. In twelfth-century Paris, if the hundreds of men standing up to their knees in the mud and slime, busy digging a massive hole, had been asked, "What are you doing?" they would have responded, "Building a cathedral!"

We conclude, then, by recognizing that, certainly, if I am now comfortable in all my relationships, if my body and my heart are at peace, if I fully perceive the meaning of my life, if I do not feel troubled by any frustration or exposed to any temptation, then I am living my chastity honestly. But if I am troubled, if I am not so sure about my feelings for a person to whom I am attracted, if I am aware of ambiguity in the feelings I have for someone, if I find it hard to manage my sexual instinct and sometimes resort to masturbation or find it hard to resist pornography; if the profound meaning of my celibacy is no longer clear to me and I live it more as a struggle than in peace, then even in all these cases it is entirely possible that I am living my chastity honestly. It is accepting that I am a story, that what defines me is not where I am now but where I want to go, where I choose to go. It is trusting in the power of the invitation, "Follow me." It is my acceptance of the gaze and the love of Jesus: "Jesus, looking at him, loved him" (Mark 10:21).

In the end, chastity is a *story*—we need to go to the end to understand the plot. The moments of struggle, failure, fatigue, and confusion are part of this story as much as the moments of light and peace, and they make the plot compelling and authentic. Both the moments of struggle and the moments of light make me more human, more supportive, more compassionate. And in the end, at the moment of death, they make me able to exult and feel alive. "Lord, let me be still alive when I will die."

CHAPTER VII

Simplicity and Prayer

Simpliciter intret et oret.
He may simply go in and pray.

RB 52.4

The first image that comes to our mind when we think of monastic life is nuns and monks wearing wide-sleeved, hooded garments (called cowls), either processing or standing, bowing and chanting in their assigned places (known as stalls) in richly decorated choirs. They gather to pray together up to seven times a day, starting before dawn with matins and ending with compline just before going to bed. Every day they devote three to five hours to this activity, which is called *opus Dei*, "the Work of God," or the "office," by singing psalms, reading Scripture, celebrating the Eucharist. Times of silence follow the readings but usually are very short—a way of catching one's breath before moving on to the next psalm. Each detail in this activity is codified, and there is very little place left for spontaneity or the expression of the individual's feelings or needs. Monastics might have to sing a joyful psalm even if in that moment they are upset or a psalm of distress even when they feel perfectly at peace. They know that during the liturgy they are expressing the feelings of the whole church, giving voice to sisters and brothers who are suffering or in need in the other parts of the globe.

Benedict's Rule devotes some nineteen chapters[1] to the meticulous description of the way in which the office should be celebrated: timing, content, posture, delays, negligence, and even exceptions such as praying the office in places located far from the chapel or while traveling (RB 50 and 51). Common liturgical prayer is at the heart of the spiritual life of the community and of each nun and monk—a principle enshrined in one of the crucial sentences of the Rule: "Nothing is to be preferred to the Work of God" (RB 43.3).[2]

By contrast, Benedict speaks very little about personal prayer and only incidentally. It would be tempting to attribute such brevity to a devaluation of personal prayer as compared to liturgical prayer. Benedictine spirituality has always flirted with formalism, as if spiritual life depended on the number of psalms sung during a given day, on the quality of the singing, on perfect timing, on the beauty of the celebration, and the splendor of vestments. Therefore, monastics, too, need to be reminded that Christianity is first of all about cultivating a personal relation of trust and love with God, as Jesus makes clear when he warns that we should avoid imitating "the hypocrites who love to pray standing in the synagogues and on the street corners to be seen by others" and the "pagans who think they will be heard because of their many words" and instead invites us to pray God our Father "in the secret" of our hearts (cf. Matt 6:5-8).

In private

Interestingly, Jesus' "secret" is suggested in Benedict's acknowledgment that there are times in which monastics might want to pray by themselves (*peculiariter*, RB 52.3) or in private (*secretius*, RB 52.4). Just as with his hesitation with regards to the quantity of

1. RB 8–20, 43, 45, 47, 50–52.
2. For a theological interpretation of this sentence, see the Conclusion: "A Spirituality for the Church."

food or drink that should be distributed to each nun or monk (RB 39 and 40), the concision of Benedict's thoughts on prayer has an obvious explanation: prayer depends on individual dispositions and therefore cannot be imposed through external regulations. All that a Rule should do about personal prayer is create the conditions that protect its freedom and its spontaneity.

At the same time, despite their brevity, the passages of the Rule that talk about prayer brim with terse and yet evocative insights on what makes it truly genuine. These remarks tend to be all the more striking as they occur almost inadvertently, as for example in chapter 52, "The Oratory of the Monastery," that deals with the place where monks should gather for their liturgical prayer:

> The oratory ought to be what it is called, and nothing else is to be done or stored there. After the Work of God, all should leave in complete silence and with reverence for God, so that a brother who may wish to pray alone will not be disturbed by the insensitivity of another. Moreover, if at other times someone chooses to pray privately, he may simply go in and pray, not in a loud voice, but with tears and heartfelt devotion. Accordingly, anyone who does not pray in this manner is not to remain in the oratory after the Work of God, as we have said; then he will not interfere with anyone else. (RB 52)

The aim of this chapter is to state that in the monastery there should be a hall especially set apart for prayer. We should not forget that Benedict was writing for sixth-century monastics before clear architectural conventions about the structure of a monastery had been established. Just as today most churches are not just places for liturgical celebrations but often host social or cultural events, so ancient monastics might have been tempted to use part of their chapel for storage or as a meeting place. The interest of this chapter, however, lies in the explanation Benedict gives for this norm. He is not concerned about the misuse of a sacred space but wants to make sure that there is a place where sisters and brothers can pray privately at any time of the day. Here, however, he drops an unexpected sentence that captures the essence of his idea of personal prayer: if someone "chooses to pray privately, he may simply go in and pray" (*simpliciter intret et oret*).

Spontaneous and genuine

The obvious meaning of this sentence is that the sister or the brother should feel free to enter the chapel directly, naturally, discreetly, and *spontaneously*. This betrays Benedict's conviction that personal prayer cannot be ritualized or codified in the same way as liturgical prayer and should be left to everyone's initiative.

However, in Latin the same adverb (*simpliciter*) can also have the ethical meaning of "sincerely, candidly, genuinely." Benedict uses it with this meaning when he says that if a monastic visiting from another community is "simply (*simpliciter*) content with what he finds, he should be received for as long a time as he wishes" (RB 61.3). In this case, the sentence quoted above can be interpreted as indicating the qualities of authentic prayer: if someone desires to pray alone in private, let him enter and pray *sincerely, candidly, genuinely*. We should therefore look for clues that explain what Benedict means by a sincere, candid, genuine, *simple* personal prayer.

The adverb *simpliciter* resonates with the etymology of the word *monk*, which comes from the Greek *monos*, "alone, only, single." A common mistake is to interpret this word as implying that a monk should lead a solitary or eremitical life. In fact, monastics started to be designated with this word not because of their "single life" but rather owing to their "single-mindedness"; that is, their choice of a lifestyle focused on the only necessary thing according to Jesus' words to Martha: "You are anxious and worried about many things. There is need of only one thing" (Luke 10:41-42)—namely, sitting at his feet and listening to him. *Monos*, therefore, refers to a lifestyle unified around the purpose of seeking God—the simplification of life is meant to facilitate the unification of the heart. Monastics yearn to acquire a heart undivided—that is, united to the Lord, according to a sentence from the psalms: "Give me an undivided heart to revere your name" (Ps 85:11, NRSV). What unifies the monastics' life is the gentle, obstinate, lifelong desire to overcome idolatry by clinging to the Lord with all their heart, all their soul, and all their strength (cf. Matt 22:37). For the prophet Jeremiah, this is the core of the covenant: "They shall be my people, and I will be their God. I will give them one heart and one way, that they may fear me always, for their own good and the good of their children after them" (Jer 32:38-39)—and Paul promises that "whoever is joined to the Lord becomes one spirit with him" (1 Cor 6:17).

Pure prayer

The meaning of *simpliciter* understood as "spontaneously" and "genuinely" to describe the characteristics of personal prayer is confirmed and expanded in the only passage of the Rule specifically devoted to this topic—namely, chapter 20, "Reverence in Prayer":

> Whenever we want to ask some favor of a powerful man, we do it humbly and respectfully, for fear of presumption. How much more important, then, to lay our petitions before the Lord God of all things with the utmost humility and sincere devotion. We must know that God regards our purity of heart and tears of compunction, not our many words. Prayer should therefore be short and pure, unless perhaps it is prolonged under the inspiration of divine grace. In community, however, prayer should always be brief; and when the superior gives the signal, all should rise together.

The title of this chapter can be misleading. Reverence suggests awe, fear, respect, regard—that is, wariness in approaching the Lord—exactly the opposite of "simply entering and praying." Instead of encouraging them to be direct, frank, natural, spontaneous, it seems to warn nuns and monks that they should tread carefully in God's presence and address him in the same way as they would with an intimidating, easily displeased monarch. A careful reading of this chapter, however, shows that in reality, Benedict is saying exactly the opposite. Whereas, he writes, powerful people should be approached humbly and respectfully (RB 20.1), God is to be addressed with humility and "*puritatis devotione*"; what RB1980 translated as "sincere devotion" might also be translated "with the devotion which is purity." A tedious but critical philological observation is needed here: the conjunction *and* in both sentences does not so much add one thing to another (humility *plus* reverence) but is meant to clarify the meaning of one word with the help of another. Thus, here Benedict is saying that powerful people should be approached with that particular kind of humility that is "reverence," whereas God should be approached with another kind of humility that is "purity." This is confirmed by the fact that this notion recurs two more times in this short chapter: our prayers are heard not thanks to our many words, but to "our purity of heart" (RB 20.3); prayer should be "short and pure" (RB 20.4).

Purity, however, is not self-explanatory, and its sexual overtones can easily taint its interpretation in this context. In fact, Benedict's understanding of this word is analogous to the "simplicity" of prayer advocated in chapter 52. The best way to understand the meaning of the inner attitude indicated here is a careful examination of the context of these two chapters. If we read them side by side, we discover that they contain some revealing parallels: monastics should not pray "in a loud voice" (RB 52.4) nor in "many words" (RB 20.3); prayer should be "with tears" (RB 52.4) or with "tears of compunction" (RB 20.3); it should be characterized by "heartfelt devotion" (*in . . . intentione cordis*, RB 52.4) and "prolonged under the inspiration of divine grace" (*ex affectu inspirationis divinae gratiae protendatur*, RB 20.4). In addition to these parallel features, chapter 52 describes prayer as being done "alone" (*peculiariter*, 52.3) and "privately" (*secretius*, 52.4), while chapter 20 says that it should be "short" (RB 20.4).

Our interpretation of this parallelism is that for Benedict, personal prayer is simple and pure when it exhibits the following qualities: (1) it is short and lasts only as long as desire fuels it; (2) it avoids using many words and instead relies on (3) compunction and tears[3] and on (4) a fervor of the heart that depends on the inspiration of divine grace. Let us look into each of these aspects in greater detail.

Short but frequent

Surely, the most baffling aspect of Benedict's teaching about prayer is that it should be short (RB 20.4)—as if to make sure it does not upset the busy monastics' timetable, take time away from their work, study, and liturgical prayer, or provide an excuse for laziness. In reality, Benedict's concern is not to belittle time dedicated to personal prayer but to make it depend on the "inspiration of divine grace" (RB 20.4). He does not say that time devoted to prayer should be restricted but that monastics should not protract it artificially. In fact, it should last only as long as joy, delight, and desire fuel it. It might be argued that in the monastic schedule, when one takes into consideration the time devoted to liturgical prayer, work, meals, and sleep, there is little extra time for personal prayer. In fact, however, monastics can pray during some of the time set apart for sleep (RB 49.4)—for example, in the afternoon, after the sixth hour (roughly midday), provided they do not bother those who are resting (RB 48.5). In Benedict's mind, however, monastics should not so much try to spend long hours in personal prayer but rather resort to heartfelt and significant short times of prayer as often as possible during the day. One of his first bits of advice to newcomers to monastic life is to pray to God to "bring . . . to perfection" whatever "good work" they begin (RB Prol. 4). Moreover he invites monastics to "devote yourselves often to prayer" (RB 4.56).

---

3. For tears, see also RB 4.57-58: "Every day with tears and sighs confess your sins to God in prayer and change from these evil ways in the future."

Not in many words

Nobody more than Benedict knows the importance of words and language or, more specifically, of Scripture and especially of the psalms for spiritual life. One of the most lyrical sentences of the Rule portrays God's voice inviting, calling, crying, warning monastics each hour of the day—in Latin the beat of the sentence is overpowering: "*Attonitis auribus audiamus divina cotidie clamans qui nos admonet vox dicens,*" "Let us open . . . our ears to the voice from heaven that every day calls out this charge" (RB Prol. 9). Now, the way in which God's voice stirs up the monk and the nun is through Scripture: "Oh, that today you would hear his voice: / Do not harden your hearts" (Ps 95:7-8) and "it is the hour now for you to awake from sleep" (Rom 13:11). And this literally happens every day and every hour because monastics keep chanting these sentences of Scripture seven times a day: "The Prophet says: 'Seven times a day I have praised you' (Ps 118[119]:164). We will fulfill this sacred number if we satisfy our obligations of service at Lauds, Prime, Terce, Sext, None, Vespers, and Compline, for it was of these hours during the day that he said: 'Seven times a day I have praised you' (Ps 118[119]:164). Concerning Vigils, the same Prophet says: 'At midnight I rose to give you praise' (Ps 118[119]:62)" (RB 16.1-4).

This means that the foundation of monastic spiritual life is, in fact, in a flood of words. There would be no knowledge of God, no monastic vocation, no spiritual life, no prayer without words. Just as in our everyday life we experience the impact of other people's words, so God touches us through the words of Scripture.[4] Commenting on the sentence from Psalm 119:50—"Your word has given me life"—the fourth-century bishop Ambrose argues that "the Word of God is the life-giving substance that feeds our soul, makes it grow, and guides it. The life of our soul grows to the extent that we welcome, understand, and embrace the Word of

---

4. For a more detailed exposition of this topic, see my book *Touched by God: The Way to Contemplative Prayer* (London: Bloomsbury, 2018).

God in our prayer."[5] Liturgical prayer is essential to spiritual life not only because of its social aspects but also as the space where God comforts, instructs, and enlightens us through his words. Scripture shapes our imagination, is stored in our memory, and becomes a reservoir we can tap into whenever we need to give voice to our trust in God, our desire and our love for him. Thus, whenever we need to pray by ourselves and in private, we easily find just the words we need to talk to God—often just one sentence from Scripture that has touched us more than others and that we savor by repeating it in our heart.

When Benedict says that personal prayer does not consist in many words, therefore, he is not denying the importance of Scripture nor opposing personal prayer to the liturgy of hours. Constant exposure to the Word of God during liturgical prayer enlivens desire and love for God—so that when we pray by ourselves we can simply let our trust, desire, and love express themselves either through repeating one sentence or even silently, in the way a lover enjoys the presence of the beloved often without needing to say anything.

Compunction and tears

For a long time I was suspicious of compunction. I had come across it in some baroque and nineteenth-century devotional literature that oozes an almost pathological pessimism, where everything is about penance and mistrust of our passions. What rescued this word and led me to see it in a completely different light is its etymology. It comes from the Latin *com* that expresses intensive force and *pungere*, "to pierce." This etymology echoes the way Scripture describes the impact of the Word of God on our hearts as, for example, in the Acts of the Apostles after Peter's proclamation of the good news: "When they heard this, they were

5. Ambrose, *Commentary on Psalm 118*, VI 1, 67 (PL 15,1282‑1283). My translation.

cut to the heart, and they asked Peter and the other apostles, 'What are we to do, my brothers?'" (Acts 2:37).

Human words often have the power to console us much more than any physical embrace, or to hurt us more than physical violence ever could. It is not surprising, therefore, that the words of Scripture should have the same or rather a much deeper effect on us when they are welcomed with living faith. According to the letter to the Hebrews, "the word of God is living and effective, sharper than any two-edged sword, penetrating even between soul and spirit, joints and marrow, and able to discern reflections and thoughts of the heart" (Heb 4:12). This is what Benedict is describing when he says that prayer should consist in the compunction of the heart: if during liturgical prayer a passage from Scripture has pierced our heart, we can feel the need to stay on in the oratory even after the celebration is over to let this God-sent feeling fulfill its work in us. This applies to all the gamut of feelings Scripture elicits in us. Indeed, if sometimes the word of God pierces our heart, more often it leaves an aftertaste of joy, peace, love—which is not surprising, since these are the signs that characterize the presence and the action of the Holy Spirit in us (cf. Gal 5:22).

In a way analogous to compunction, we have become wary of tears in prayer. Crying in itself is not a proof that our feelings are genuine. We can simply be wallowing in self-pity, which is not really healthy. Benedict refers to tears within a well-attested tradition that can be traced back to Jesus' sentence: "Blessed are they who mourn, for they will be comforted" (Matt 5:4). The Greek word for "mourning with tears" is *penthountes* from which comes the word *penthos*, a synonym of compunction: when God touches our heart through his word, we can experience tears that are caused by a mixture of repentance for sin and joy for having been forgiven. This means that only certain kinds of tears are the manifestation of the type of prayer that Benedict calls pure, as we can learn from Peter's example in the Gospels. We see him shedding tears after his denial of Jesus, but Matthew makes clear that this was no *penthos*, no compunction: "Then Peter remembered the word that Jesus had spoken: 'Before the cock crows you will deny me three times.' He went out and began to weep bitterly" (Matt 26:75). These are tears of guilt and misery. Peter's access to authentic compunction only happens later on, after Jesus' resurrection, at the Lake of Tiberias. What eventually pierces Peter's heart is not a reproach, but Jesus' patient, delicate, persistent poking and the pricking (*punctio*) of his insistent questioning: "Do you love me?" (John 21:15-18). This question is not meant to inspire guilt but is almost playful. In this scene, Jesus comes across as vulnerable, almost needy: he desires our love, our desire, our trust. Patiently he cuts through our defense mechanisms and our fear of him until he elicits from us the declaration that seals our bond with him: "Lord, you know everything; you know that I love you" (John 21:17). It is a compunction that does not hurt us but liberates us from guilt by giving us access to authentic self-knowledge—it reveals to us that we are loved not despite our weaknesses but because of them and that however beset by contradictions, our heart is miraculously capable of loving the Lord.

The intention of the heart

Benedict's restraint concerning personal prayer is based on the deeply held conviction that the *intentio cordis* (RB 52.4), the intention of the heart, in prayer should depend on the inspiration of the Holy Spirit. This resonates with his assertion that monastics should pray with all humility, *cum omni humilitate* (RB 20.2). The link between humility, Holy Spirit, and spontaneity in prayer is explained in chapter 7, "Humility" (the longest of the entire Rule), dedicated to the core virtue of Benedictine asceticism. In this chapter, Benedict compares growth in spiritual life to the climbing of a ladder, where progress consists in deeper inner freedom and delight. Once we reach the last step of this ladder, the twelfth, we discover that Benedict is describing the same humility that, according to chapter 20, fuels authentic prayer: gradually monastics are granted access to a spontaneity in life and in prayer whereby, thanks to the Holy Spirit, they begin to "delight in virtue" no longer out of fear but "as though naturally . . . out of love for Christ" (*sed amore Christi et consuetudine ipsa bona et delectatione virtutum*) (RB 7.68-69). This idea echoes the conclusion of the Prologue, where Benedict affirms that advancement in conversion leads monastics to "run on the path of God's commandments, our hearts overflowing with the inexpressible delight of love" (RB Prol. 49).

This explains why personal prayer cannot be codified. It belongs to the field of love, of the heart that widens thanks to the delight and sweetness of being with the Lord and of tuning in with the inspiration of the Holy Spirit. Benedict is often portrayed as an austere legislator, but his purpose is to teach monastics authentic self-knowledge and the discernment that gives access to inner freedom and spontaneity. This recurs in other passages of the Rule as, for example, in the chapter on Lent, where decisions about which practices to take up are "of [the monastic's] own will" (*propria voluntate*), should be accompanied by "the joy of the Holy Spirit" (*gaudio Sancti Spiritus*), and should feed his or her "joy and spiritual longing" (*cum spiritalis desiderii gaudio*) (RB 49.6). Anyone familiar with the prominence of obedience in Benedictine monasticism cannot avoid noticing the unusual mention of *propria voluntate*, "of his own will," in this chapter. It shows that Benedict's purpose is not to obliterate the free will of monks and nuns but help them to trust the most authentic impulses of their hearts (*intentio cordis*). As in many other spiritual traditions (notably Ignatian spirituality), joy, delight, sweetness, and desire are the signs that our inspiration to act or to pray really comes from God. All Benedict wants is to teach monks and nuns to become alert to the presence and the action of the Holy Spirit in their lives.

The great lesson of Benedict's approach to personal prayer, then, is that it is the necessary antidote against legalism and formalism and a litmus test of the authenticity of monastic vocation. Just as monastics are called to be *monoi*—that is, "single-minded" in their search for God in the midst of their activities—so their prayer should become more and more "simple"—that is, spontaneous and genuine. Even in a monastery it is possible to forget the Lord and perform daily activities routinely, distractedly, or anxiously—and this is unavoidable because it is part of what it means to be human. Short but frequent moments of personal prayer should punctuate the day so as to check the intention of our heart, redirect our desire to the Lord, rekindle our motivation—or simply rejoice in the Lord's love.

CHAPTER VIII

Experiencing God

*At a certain point after the resurrection the apostles
ceased to receive experiences of the particular human
being Jesus of Nazareth and started to receive a
slightly different experience which had to do with, but
was not the same as, their previous experience of Jesus.*

James Alison[1]

Any spirituality that aims to be more than a pure abstraction
must confront the question of the experience of God, an experience that is not only communal but personal; not only mediated
through texts, teachers, and rites, but in some way immediate and
direct; not only formal, but felt; not just external, but internal.
Countless ambiguities lurk behind each of the aspects just listed,
but this challenge must be faced boldly, because these aspects
characterize many spiritual paths in the Christian tradition and in
other religions. According to these paths, advancement in the life
of faith means greater access to a personal, interior, experienced,
direct contact with God; the spirituality of the monastic should
rely not only on instruction received from the outside but on the
ability to listen to the inner teaching of the Holy Spirit—that is,

1. James Alison, *Knowing Jesus* (Springfield, IL: Templegate, 1994), 26.

on an understanding of God and of reality more profound than what is obtained through the external mediation of rites and texts.

What follows is a critical evaluation of this approach. We'll consider the notions of *interiority* and *experience*, note some misunderstandings of this way of reflecting on spiritual life, and then try to specify what an authentically Christian spirituality entails.

Interiority and experience

When we speak of the self, of interiority, we are often unconsciously conditioned by the conception of these realities developed in modern thought in the wake of Descartes and Kant. In modernity, the self (that is, one's interiority) is conceived as pure thought that is independent of all that is historical, contingent, practical, or interrelational. External reality is reduced to what can be known by the subject. The "I" is privatized and becomes the arbiter and the source of values.

For this reason, modernity's great interest in mysticism, interiority, and spirituality is somehow dubious. A classic work in this regard is the American psychologist and philosopher William James's book, *The Varieties of Religious Experience.*[2] James considers religious or spiritual experience to be a feeling of joy and strength that transfigures human life. However, a significant aspect of his description of religious experience is the absence of any social or interrelational element and even of any precise and defined relationship to God. Even God becomes secondary to experience. Only experience is considered important and worthy of interest.

This trend is prominent in modernity, but it echoes a broader phenomenon that has always been present in both Christian and non-Christian spirituality, which we might call "spiritualism." This term points to the tendency to believe that interiority gives access

2. William James, *The Varieties of Religious Experience: A Study in Human Nature* (New York: Penguin, 1982; orig. ed. New York: Longmans, Green, and Co., 1902).

to a mode of knowledge of divinity greater than what is obtained through any form of external mediation—texts, rites, teachers, communities, traditions. By accessing interiority, by knowing oneself, one also acquires a direct perception of divinity. External mediation is given, at most, a preliminary and provisional role to support one's weakness, but true knowledge is interior.

On trends of this kind in Christian spirituality, Hans Urs von Balthasar wrote, "[The mysticism of Francis de Sales and John of the Cross] was, primarily, not a mysticism of service in the Church, but one of subjective experience, individual states. The mystical states are, of course, the objects of John of the Cross' and Teresa of Avila's descriptions; roughly speaking, the external objects are derived from the state which reveals them. . . . [T]he accent is always on experience rather than on God: for the nature of God is a subject for a theological specialist."[3]

Experience (what I "feel") takes its place above its object (God) and all attention is focused on it. To prevent this drawback, therefore, it is important to look for a more authentic notion of experience.

In his classic work, *The Christian Experience*, Jean Mouroux explains the drawbacks of forms of spirituality that focus too much on experience. The risk is a reductive notion of experience that is understood either in an "empirical" way (experience is something one passively undergoes) or in an "idealist" way (experience is the expression of mind's activity, a purely mental construct). Mouroux proposes to broaden the notion of experience when he writes,

> At least three meanings must be given to the verb 'to experi-
> ence.' Experience may take the form of an act, and this kind
> of experience is active and personal, because the person pos-
> its the actual reality of the experience. Then again it may
> take the form of a state that is merely endured, and this kind

3. Hans Urs von Balthasar, "Theology and Sanctity," in *The Word Made Flesh: Explorations in Theology*, vol. 1, trans. A. V. Littledale with Alexander Dru (San Francisco: Ignatius Press, 1989), 190, 192.

of experience is passive, unfree, undifferentiated, and as little personal as anything can be. Thirdly, it may take the form of a state that is received with welcome, and this kind of experience is still passive, but it is enveloped within a magnificent act of freedom.[4]

In this latter sense, experience is authentic only when the person understands herself in relation to the world, to herself, and to God.[5] Mouroux provides the example of one's experience of another person. I can experience the other in an active way, either positively or negatively, liking her or disliking her; or the other is "something resistant, an obstacle" which hinders me, and I experience her in a passive way, independent of my initiative, in spite of myself. But both these forms of experience are reductive. The other is either reduced to what I can perceive or just something that imposes itself on me.

A more authentic form of experience, therefore, is what Mouroux calls "received": I open myself to the other either to accept or to refuse her.[6] The fact that experience depends on something that comes from outside does not mean that it is passive. I truly know the other not when I wait for her to impose herself upon me, but when I go and encounter her, investing myself actively in this encounter with all that I am.

This brief *excursus* on the notions of interiority and experience helps us see how reductive both the approach of modernity and that of spiritualism are. A transparent, immediately accessible, neutral self that is the source of all other evidence simply does not exist.[7]

4. Jean Mouroux, *The Christian Experience: An Introduction to a Theology*, trans. George Lamb (New York: Sheed and Ward, 1954), 12–13.

5. Mouroux, 10.

6. Mouroux, 13.

7. Cf. Jean-Yves Lacoste, *The Appearing of God*, trans. Oliver O'Donovan (London: Oxford University Press, 2018; orig. ed. Paris: Neuf études, 2008), 21: "An 'ego,' or consciousness, with powers of comprehensive perception . . . [is a] larger-than-life ego [that] does not belong to a human being."

The more we know our self ("self-knowledge"), the more we have to recognize that it is an enigma, a tangle of contradictions. The great master of self-knowledge, Augustine, declared in his *Confessions* that he had become a great puzzle to himself.[8] Interiority, the self, did not appear to him as a certain and clear knowledge, but as a riddle, a *quaestio*.[9]

Knowing oneself by knowing God

Because interiority is mysterious, elusive, and problematic, great caution is required when dealing with "inner" experiences, whatever they may be. One cannot accept too easily the idea of an immediate, inner knowledge of God that is autonomous and superior to mediated knowledge, which many forms of spiritualism claim to offer. The most authentic Christian spiritual tradition has always been inclined to be wary of these inner experiences, subjecting them to careful discernment.

It is naive to think that since interior spiritual experiences are received passively—that is, they are not actively procured—then they necessarily have a supernatural cause.[10] Without reference to an objective, external criterion, there is no way to discern whether an interior experience has a supernatural origin, and the possibilities of self-deception are widely recognized throughout the spiritual tradition and further expanded with the help of the more recent field of psychology.

It is here that theology intervenes to affirm that, being made in the image of God, the human person knows herself only by

---

8. Augustine, *Confessions*, 4,4,9.

9. Jean-Luc Marion, "*Mihi magna quaestio factus sum*: The Privilege of Unknowing," *The Journal of Religion* 85 (2005): 1–24. Cf. Luigi Gioia, "Il carattere teologale, storico ed ecclesiale dell'identità personale in Agostino," *Gregorianum* 95 (2014) 3: 487–509.

10. Henri de Lubac, *Mistica e mistero cristiano* (Milan: Jaca Book, 1978), 20; orig. ed. *La mystique et les mystiques* (Paris: Desclée de Brouwer, 1965).

knowing God or, rather, only through God's self-revelation. Augustine, from the first works written immediately after his conversion, recognizes that knowledge of himself and knowledge of God are interwoven. *Noverim me, noverim te*, he already affirmed in the *Soliloquies*—"I want to know myself that I may know you."[11] He assigns priority to knowledge of God and will emphasize this increasingly in his later works. Augustine compares interiority to a mirror: I know myself only when I see within me the reflection of the one in whose image I was created, God the Trinity: "They who see in this mirror and in this enigma, as it is permitted in this life to see are . . . those who see this as an image of God."[12] Those who seek to know themselves without first knowing God "see indeed a mirror, but do not see God in the mirror."[13]

Augustine expresses the same truth in another way when he writes that the self, the interiority of the human person, is an enigma or, rather, an obscure allegory.[14] Interiority is like a mirror, an enigma, an allegory; that is, it needs to be deciphered, to be interpreted: "The person who is properly self-aware is aware of obscurity, darkness, a crabbed striving for representation, something crying out for interpretation."[15]

Not only do we not have access to an autonomous knowledge of God solely through interiority, but we cannot even have access to our interiority (our "self" or our "heart") without something from the outside that guides us, that "interprets" us. Henri de Lubac wrote significantly in this regard that "Christian spirituality [is]

11. Augustine, *Soliloquies*, II,i,1. Cf. Gioia, "Il carattere teologale," 487–509.

12. Augustine, *On the Trinity* (*De Trinitate*) 15,23,44, trans. Arthur West Haddan, in Philip Schaff, ed., *The Nicene and Post-Nicene Fathers of the Christian Church*, vol. III (Grand Rapids: Wm. B. Eerdmans Publishing Co., 1956), 223. (Minor revisions have been made here and in the next quoted passage to update outdated language in the original English translation.—Trans.)

13. Augustine, *On the Trinity*, 15,24,44, Haddan, 223.

14. Augustine, *On the Trinity*, 15,9,15, Haddan, 207.

15. John Cavadini, "The Darkest Enigma: Reconsidering the Self in Augustine's Thought," *Augustinian Studies* 38 (2007): 113–132, 125.

essentially an understanding of Sacred Scripture. . . . The mystical or spiritual understanding of Scripture and the mystical or spiritual life are, in the end, the same thing."[16] This sentence means that I know myself by knowing God, and the better I know God, the better I know myself. This is why the word of God opens the way to interiority, to allow us to decipher the enigma, the *quaestio*, the allegory that is our self, and to interpret it. The meaning of this connection must be explored in all its consequences: "If we are in search of ourselves, if we are a riddle to ourselves, it is because our true identity does not emerge except in the recognition of our relationship with God, which constitutes us in the most intimate part of ourselves. . . . Knowledge of God proves to be inseparable from self-knowledge. The mediation of Scripture proves necessary for sinful people to rediscover the path of interiority and allow them to be enlightened by God about themselves."[17]

The necessary mediations

As we noted above, true experience is not purely passive, nor is it a construction of the spirit. Rather, it consists in opening ourselves to what is given to us, in encountering what comes to us. Every authentic experience requires a conversion, an investment that is not only intellectual but involves all of oneself, of one's whole person and of one's whole life. In this way we understand a luminous affirmation of de Lubac in his book *History and Spirit*, regarding the true meaning of the method of biblical exegesis known as mystical or spiritual sense—that is, the only one that approaches Scripture as God speaking to me now:

---

16. Henri de Lubac, *Mistica e mistero cristiano*, 26.

17. Isabelle Bochet, "Une identité reçue de Dieu," in *Le firmament de l'Écriture: L'herméneutique augustinienne* (Paris: Institut d'études augustiniennes, 2004), 308. Cf. 326: "Scripture . . . is perfectly appropriate as a mediation between us and ourselves, between our *forma obscura* and our *forma lucida* or even between our *deformis forma* and our *forma formosa*."

> The veil will not be removed from our eyes as long as we are
> not turned toward the Lord. *The passage from letter to spirit
> is the same movement of* metanoia *(conversion)*. . . . [T]his
> conversion is never something acquired once and for all. . . .
> We will not forget, therefore, that understanding is not here
> a matter of cleverness of mind, even a mind illumined by
> God, but of purity of heart, of uprightness, and if simplicity,
> together with a certain "lightness": a heart weighed down
> by love of material goods is incapable of discerning in Scrip-
> ture the mystery of its salvation.[18]

Access to the spiritual sense of Scripture—that is, to the word
of God as an event, to the possibility of listening to God who
speaks to me now—and to the spiritual or interior life are the same
thing; they constitute the same movement. Understanding the
Word and understanding the self are linked. It is therefore clear
why spiritual life depends on the word of God, access to interiority
relies on ecclesial mediations. Indeed, "the word of God" here is to
be understood not simply as "the Bible" but as the act, the spiritual
event that occurs every time that, through Scripture, we listen to
the Father through the Son in the Holy Spirit. When this happens, the Word calls us, it is effective, it converts and transforms
us. When we say "the word of God," we imply the trinitarian
mystery; we also imply the church, the community of those who
are summoned by this Word—the *creatura Verbi*, as Luther called
it; and we imply the *traditio* through which the Scripture reaches
us and the ministry through which it is proclaimed in all times and
places and is interpreted (hence the role of ecclesial mediation).

Christian spiritual life is necessarily trinitarian—that is, the
work of the Holy Spirit who unites us to Christ and cries out
"Abba" in our hearts. It is necessarily ecclesial: the love of God is

---

18. Henri de Lubac, *History and Spirit: The Understanding of Scripture according to Origen*, trans. Anne Englund Nash (San Francisco: Ignatius Press, 2007),
362, 265–366. Emphasis mine.

poured into our hearts through the Spirit who is given to us, and in the Son all are brothers and sisters.

No spirituality without theology

This explains the mutual dependence of theology and spirituality and the reason why any progress in spiritual life must be accompanied by a serious study of theology. Theology is one of the charisms within the life of the church that helps us understand and assimilate the Word that we hear, celebrate, and live, and upon which a healthy and balanced spiritual life depends. At the same time, the dynamic proper to the Word is interiorization, personal adherence, the growth of the fruits of the Spirit. If theology does not preserve its mooring in spirituality, it ceases to be inspired by the living Word, to be a spiritual event, and becomes instead the guardian and interpreter of a dead letter. De Lubac writes, "Separated from the mystery [that is 'theology'] received by the believer, spirituality becomes empty or degraded. Conversely, separated from spirituality . . . the mystery [that is theology] is exteriorized, it risks becoming lost in arid formulas and empty abstractions. . . . There is fertilization, because theology always must nourish the spiritual life, or the process of internalization. . . . In other words, spirituality continually internalizes theology: it owes its life to it, and it allows theology to become alive in the one who welcomes it."[19]

And in fact, the divorce between theology and spirituality[20] has resulted in a divorce between theology and holiness. To recall the well-known observation of Hans Urs von Balthasar, "As time went on, theology at prayer [literally, 'theology on one's knees'] was superseded by theology at the desk."[21] Of course, neither Augustine nor Anselm nor Thomas Aquinas wrote their works while literally

19. Henri de Lubac, *Mistica e mistero cristiano*, 21.

20. Vandenbroucke, "Le divorce entre théologie et mystique, 372–387.

21. Balthasar, "Theology and Sanctity," 208.

on their knees, but the image suggests that their theology was an act of adoration, nourished not only by knowledge but also by love and desire.[22] For these great doctors, the very expression "spiritual theology" would have been incomprehensible. Augustine's *De Trinitate*, for example, is not a treatise, but a mystagogy through which the readers are led to recognize in the Trinity the most profound meaning of their own existence and thus understand that they can know themselves only by letting themselves be known and loved by God; driven by this love, the readers pass from the forgetfulness of God to the *memoria Dei,* "the remembrance of God"; that is, they discover that the roots of their being are in God and that they find themselves only by converting themselves to the one by whom they were created, turning to the Father through the Son in the Holy Spirit.

Theology, then, is, entirely inseparable from a spirituality that rediscovers the vital importance of the Trinity, of Christ and of the church: these are the framework that gives spirituality its shape and life. Spirituality becomes indistinguishable from theology only when we truly trust, love, and desire God—and for that reason we become all the more eager to know him.

No spirituality without community

What does monasticism bring to the theology and spirituality of the whole church? To speak of "monastic spiritual theology" doesn't mean inquiring about the kind of spiritual theology that

---

22. Balthasar, "Theology and Sanctity," 206–207: "Their theology is essentially an act of adoration and prayer. . . . Christian dogmatics must express the fact that one whose thinking is dictated by faith is in a constant relationship of prayer with its object. . . . Prayer is the *realistic* attitude in which the mystery must be approached: obedient faith, the 'presuppositionless,' is the attitude where theology is concerned, because it corresponds to the tabula rasa of love, in which the heart awaits all and anticipates nothing. This attitude, which is that of prayer, is never superseded or outdistanced by the attitude demanded by knowledge."

works best for monastics. Rather, it is an attempt to single out aspects of monastic wisdom that can be useful for the whole church especially with regards to the balance between theology and spirituality, between the word of God (as an event) and life, between individualism and fellowship, between legalism and the *dilatatio cordis*, "the widening of the heart."

In the description of the various types of monastics, in the first chapter of his Rule, Benedict outlines the characteristics of hermits or anchorites: "[They] have come through the test of living in a monastery for a long time, and have passed beyond the first fervor of monastic life. Thanks to the help and guidance of many, they are now trained to fight against the devil. They have built up their strength and go from the battle line in the ranks of their brothers and sisters to the single combat of the desert. Self-reliant now, without the support of another, they are ready with God's help to grapple single-handed with the vices of body and mind" (RB 1.3-5).

The greatest temptation in the Christian life is to seek access to a deeper spirituality by isolating oneself from others or from the world, closing in on oneself, relying only on one's own discernment. To be sure, the vocation to the eremitic life exists, and the history of monasticism attests that it has been lived in a fruitful way by many men and women over the centuries; but before being able to undertake it, one needs to have carried out the difficult and long journey of self-understanding.

Spirituality and self-understanding are synonymous. There is no spiritual life without descending into one's heart—that is, without interiority and self-reflection; but as soon as one looks into her own heart, she must learn the difficult art of discernment of thoughts, of managing emotions, of confrontation with the subconscious. The ever-more fruitful interweaving of spirituality and psychology of the last half century is rooted in the most ancient monastic and spiritual tradition and is widely found even in non-Christian forms of spirituality.

The wisdom of the monastic tradition distilled in the Rule of Benedict intends to resolutely lead the monastic on this journey of self-reflection. Beginning with the prologue, the external norm is presented as a necessity in the service of widening of the heart (we could say "inner growth") and of progress in the life of faith thanks to which we reach an adhesion to God and to God's commandments that is spontaneous, free, and heartfelt, marked by *inenarrabili dilectionis dulcedine*, "the inexpressible delight of love" (RB Prol. 49).

But to achieve this aim in a sound and safe way, Benedictine monastic wisdom uses a series of robust mediations: the word of God, the *opus Dei*, the community, the abbot or abbess, the holy fathers, and the Rule itself. All of the demanding discipline relating to the celebration of the Liturgy of the Hours, fraternal life, work, eating, sleeping, and reading may seem at times to excessively and unduly accentuate the form, the external framework, and it's true that the most frequent distortions of monasticism—perhaps especially of the Benedictine variety—are formalism, ritualism, or aestheticism. But in reality, such discipline is entirely at the service of progress in conversion and faith, growth in charity, the flowering of the fruits of the Holy Spirit, the development of "good zeal," and life according to the Spirit (cf. Gal 5:16-25).

Monastic life is thus understood as a discipline totally at the service of an objective spirituality—that is, one that is rooted in the mystery received in faith, by listening to the Word, celebrating the liturgy, living fraternal life, hospitality, and work. The dimension of interiority is rarely made explicit. It is often taken for granted and can be unearthed only through an interpretation of the Rule that helps to recognize it behind the pervasive and sometimes tedious normative aspects of Benedictine monasticism.

CHAPTER IX

The Word of God and Monasticism

*Since the Church always needs signs and reminders of
its nature when it is tempted to slip into the tribalism
of race and class or "agenda," the dependence of the
monastic community simply on the Word is a gift to
the Church's self-critical energy.*

Rowan Williams[1]

The most rewarding method for approaching familiar questions
is by engaging with the interlocutors that challenge us the most.
With regards to the relation of the monastic tradition with the
word of God, nobody seems more apt to play this role than the
great Reformed theologian Karl Barth (d. 1968). His fourteen-
volume *Church Dogmatics* (1932–1967) consists in a tightly-woven
reformulation of all the main tenets of Christian doctrine as the
unfolding of the dynamism of the word of God—that is, of the act
through which God reveals himself to us. No aspect of Christian
life is left undisturbed in the course of Barth's uncompromising
and sustained questioning. He freely, acutely, probingly—and
often fiercely—confronts all Christian denominations, including

---

1. Williams, *The Way of St Benedict*, 64.

and maybe especially the very Reformed tradition to which he belonged and in which he ministered as a pastor. He is not tender toward many aspects of Catholicism either, but this has not prevented a wide and deep reception of his thought in Catholic theology, spearheaded by the seminal works of theologians such as Hans Urs von Balthasar[2] and Hans Küng,[3] and memorably acknowledged by Pope Paul VI during Barth's 1967 visit to Rome.[4]

The renewal of Benedictine monasticism

Benedictine monasticism has faced Barth's probing questioning as well. Indeed, it invited such questioning at a strategic juncture of the history of the Benedictine order, as it undertook the task of rethinking its charism in the wake of the *aggiornamento* to which the whole church had been summoned by the Second Vatican Council. A commission led by the abbot of Montserrat, Gabriel Brasó, sent a letter to Karl Barth on February 15, 1966, asking him "to offer short responses to three questions: 1) what do you think of the nature of the monastic life (not the religious life generally, but specifically monastic life)?; 2) what do you believe that the church expects today from the monks?; and 3) where has, in your opinion, the *aggiornamento* of monasticism come into existence, which direction should it follow, and by which basic rules is it spread?"[5] Only ten days later, Barth replied to this request with a

2. Hans Urs von Balthasar, *The Theology of Karl Barth: Exposition and Interpretation*, trans. Edward T. Oakes (San Francisco: Communio Books, Ignatius Press, 1992).

3. Hans Küng, *Justification: The Doctrine of Karl Barth and a Catholic Reflection*, trans. Thomas Collins, Edward E. Tolk, and David Granskou (New York: Nelson, 1964).

4. Cf. Karl Barth, *Ad Limina Apostolorum: An Appraisal of Vatican II*, trans. Keith R. Crim (Richmond: John Knox Press, 1968).

5. Cf. Greg Peters, *Reforming the Monastery: Protestant Theologies of the Religious Life* (Eugene, OR: Cascade Books, 2013), 104.

little-known letter[6] that provides us with a sound and lucid theological frame for our topic.

For him, the charism of monastic life lies in its exemplary role with regards to the life of the church. Monasticism does not exist for its own sake, but it is a ministry whereby monks and nuns try to be brothers and sisters to each other in a special way and thus become brothers and sisters of all Christians and of all people. Their life is meaningful insofar as it gives witness to God "in the world, towards the world, and for the world." However, in the final paragraph of the letter Barth confronts some crucial conditions on which monastic life "stands or falls," which he considers to be the most serious threat to the ministry and to the exemplary role and witness of monastic life. A council, Barth says, can invite the church to *aggiornamento*, that is the "renewal," but this renewal can effectively be guided only by the word of God. In fact, renewal is not an episodic aspect of the life of the church or of monasticism in particular, but it belongs to their existence and defines their essence: "Their particular monastic existence stands and falls by the fact that their Lord, who is always faithful to himself and to this extent also to them, wills them, establishes them and orders them anew at every moment and in every situation, and that their existence, for its part, is always open, willing and ready to live anew by his free mercy and to be newly obedient only to his free command."[7]

Anyone even remotely acquainted with Barth's thought instantly detects here the key tenets of his ecclesiology and more generally of his understanding of Christian life as an *event* incessantly triggered by the living, active, and effective word of God—that is, God in the act of speaking to us.[8]

---

6. The letter can be found in Karl Barth, *Visioni attuali sulla vita monastica* (Barcelona: Abadía de Montserrat, 1966), 43f.

7. Barth, *Visioni attuali sulla vita monastica*, 44.

8. Cf. Eberhard Jüngel, *God's Being Is in Becoming: The Trinitarian Being of God in the Theology of Karl Barth*, trans. John Webster (Edinburgh: T&T Clark, 2001).

Barth had given the traits of the monastic charism outlined in this short letter a more extensive treatment eleven years earlier, in a section of the *Church Dogmatics* (vol. IV.2)[9] specifically devoted to this question in the context of the life of the reconciled person. Barth's theological reading of monastic tradition in the light of the word of God in this text can be summarized around the three key ideas highlighted in his letter to the Benedictine abbots—that is (1) *ministry*, (2) *exemplary character* and (3) *monastic life as event* or, as he says here, as *action*.

Potential shortcomings

For Barth, monastic life can be seen as Christian only insofar as (1) it strives to embody the ministerial aspect and the solidarity with all Christians and all humanity that is essential to Christian life.[10] Then (2) Barth acknowledges the exemplary role fulfilled by monasticism in the course of history as a "highly responsible and effective protest and opposition to the world and not least to a worldly church"[11] that had lost her eschatological impetus and become more and more secularized.[12] A form of life is indeed Christian only if it is in the world, toward the world, and for the world, but precisely this commitment involves acceptance of a conflict[13] and retreat[14] as the reclaiming of a freedom for God and for one's fellows.[15] The fruitfulness of this attitude has been testified by the many influential movements of reform born within the monastic environment.[16]

Just as in the letter written to the abbots and abbesses, however, in this text, too, the ministry and the exemplary role of monasti-

9. Cf. Peters, *Reforming the Monastery*, 99.

10. Karl Barth, *Church Dogmatics* IV/ 2, ed. G. W. Bromiley, trans. Harold Knight (London: T&T Clark, 1958), 14. (Henceforth, Barth, CD IV/2.)

11. Barth, CD IV/2, 13.

12. Barth, CD IV/2, 15.

13. Barth, CD IV/2, 16.

14. Barth, CD IV/2, 14.

15. Barth, CD IV/2, 16.

16. Barth, CD IV/2, 14.

cism (3) should rely not on institutional settings but on a conscious and constant dependence on God's action—that is, on a renewed and actual hearing of the word of God. This point relates to some features of monastic tradition that Barth sees as threats to its ministry in the church and in the world.

First of all, in relation to the world, it would be naive to think that physical withdrawal alone can make monks and nuns free. "One thing is sure," says Barth, "that even in his hut or cave the hermit will never be free from the most dangerous representative of the world, i.e., himself."[17] For the monk or nun, for the monastic community just as for the church as a whole, the greatest threat is not the world without, but the world within, which Barth describes elsewhere under the headings of secularization, self-glorification, and sacralization. From an evangelical viewpoint, *secularization* is the process whereby the salt loses its savor[18] and the church uncritically adopts what seems to be the most urgent and sacred need in its own particular environment.[19] *Self-glorification* has been the scourge precisely of the forms and reforms of monasticism most widespread, successful, and therefore influential. It leads to self-assertion and to a developed consciousness of oneself[20] and to communities that start trying to be important and powerful within the world instead of serving the world.[21] Finally, the greatest of these threats, as far as monasticism is concerned, has probably always been that which Barth labels *sacralization*, that is, the "transmutation of the lordship of Jesus Christ into the vanity of a Christianity enamored only of itself and its traditions, confessions and institutions."[22]

That the church in general and monastic communities in particular should be exposed to these threats is the unavoidable

17. Barth, CD IV/2, 12.

18. Karl Barth, *Church Dogmatics* IV/ 1, ed. G. W. Bromiley, trans. Harold Knight (London: T&T Clark, 1956), 668. (Henceforth, Barth, CD IV/1).

19. Barth, CD IV/1, 667.

20. Barth, CD IV/1, 668.

21. Barth, CD IV/1, 669.

22. Barth, CD IV/1, 670.

downside of their call to be in the *world*, toward the *world*, and for the *world*;[23] it is "integral to what the Church is on earth, to what its commission is."[24] In the course of history, these threats have caused the decline of countless communities and have often seriously obscured their witness. If, however, these threats have not been able to prevail, it is thanks to what Barth calls the "strange persistence"[25] of the communities that are upheld by the word of God.[26] The word of God "has always been heard in its one, original and authentic form where Scripture has again made itself to be heard and created hearers for itself."[27] This has happened because Jesus in his Holy Spirit remains within his community.[28]

Another of Barth's critical remarks is that despite the potential positive aspects of the monastic approach to sex, property, and speech, institutional vows tended to become the expression of a "mechanical sealing off" of these spheres,[29] as if this could be enough to neutralize the latter's disruptive potential in Christian life. Similarly, with regard to the idea that obeying people (the spiritual father, the abbot, the staretz, and so on) is obeying God, he warns against the danger of institutionalizing these gifts and thus potentially conflating human and divine action.[30] Finally, Barth evokes one of the main criticisms the Protestant tradition has always levelled against monasticism, aimed at what he calls "optimism":[31] "It is a pity that the final sentence in [Benedict's Rule] is as follows: *Facientibus haec regna patebunt superna* ["The eternal Kingdom will open to those who do this"]. This cannot be admitted for a moment. The statement must be resolutely reformulated. It is not because and as they do this that the *regna superna*

23. Barth, *Visioni attuali sulla vita monastica*, 43.
24. Barth, CD IV/1, 670.
25. Barth, CD IV/1, 673.
26. Barth, CD IV/1, 674.
27. Barth, CD IV/1, 674.
28. Barth, CD IV/1, 675.
29. Barth, CD IV/2, 15.
30. Barth, CD IV/2, 17.
31. Barth, CD IV/2, 14.

will open up to them. It is because and as the *regna superna* are opened up to them in the death of Jesus Christ that they will do this in the power of his resurrection."[32]

Strange persistence

However, far from representing a dismissal of monastic ministry and charism, these critical observations are meant to emphasize the secret of the extraordinary fruitfulness of monasticism in Christianity, of its "strange persistence,"[33] namely, the role played by the word of God in monastic tradition.

It is true that Pelagianism—and even more so, its offspring, usually gathered under the loose label of "semi-Pelagianism"—originated and thrived in monastic circles. Pelagius (d. 418) himself is thought to have been a British monk, and traces of semi-Pelagianism can be detected in Cassian's writings, which decisively shaped Western monastic spirituality (d. 435). It is also true that the practical nature of Benedict's Rule can unwittingly fall into the slippery slope of transactional language. Barth, however, does not believe that these blunders compromise the overall value of monastic tradition, and he dismisses the ubiquitous misperception of early Protestant anti-monastic apologetics on this point when he states: "This sequence [from works to reward] . . . was certainly suppressed in the history of monasticism, and even denied and contested in its forms. . . . [Thus] we have always to learn from monasticism that it derives from faith and that necessarily in faith it has to do with discipleship, sanctification, concretion, brotherhood and love. Those who recognize what has been revealed for the world and for them in the resurrection of Jesus Christ will do this in the power of his resurrection."[34]

---

32. Barth, CD IV/2, 18. In fact, this sentence is not in RB but sums up the content of the last sentence of RB.

33. Barth, CD IV/1, 673.

34. Barth, CD IV/2, 18.

Then, in the following sentence, revealingly, he refers to monasticism as an *action* three times: "We should [not] suppress or neglect *this action*. . . . We see clearly that *this action*, put in the right context, must not on any account be suppressed or neglected, but given its proper place. . . . *This action* deserve[s] our serious consideration in detail."[35]

Monastic life as action

In Barth's thought, no greater theological value and potential can be attributed to an aspect of Christian life than calling it an *action* (or an *event*). In the sentence just quoted, this move is meant to explain how, despite its potential shortcomings, monastic tradition has managed to preserve its authenticity and hence its fruitfulness for the life of the church—that is, "its desire and aim [to be] a concrete individual and collective sanctification, a teleological concretion of the Christian status, a practical and regulated brotherhood, and all this in the service of concrete and total love."[36]

Now, the only means for Christian life to preserve this living character, to remain an action, an event, something constantly happening anew, a constant renewal (or *aggiornamento*), is its openness to the word of God.

Here, it is vital to be aware of the distinction Barth assumes between the word of God and Scripture. A little analogy with our human interactions might help us to grasp this distinction. Speech is inherently relational. A word makes sense only insofar as it establishes, sanctions, expresses, clarifies a relation. What gives weight to a human word is the person speaking it and the extent to which I have access through this word to this person. Thus, if a friend writes a letter to me, this writing brings me joy because the love expressed in it is that of a person I care for and who cares for me. If a total stranger was to read the same letter,

---

35. Barth, CD IV/2, 18. Emphasis mine.
36. Barth, CD IV/2, 18.

he might understand its content and appreciate its style, but that would not bring him any joy because the letter is not addressed to him, and it does not refer to an actual relationship for him. Thus Scripture becomes alive only as it is received as word, as *the* Word addressed to us. The written words (Scripture) speak to me only if and as God himself speaks to me when I read or hear them (word of God). Properly speaking, therefore, the word of God is the event (or the action) whereby some human limited and fallible words become the medium or the occasion through which God addresses me, reveals himself to me, reconciles me to himself, and establishes me in fellowship with all those who have been reached by this same address.

This linear analogy, however, does not take into account the fact that God is invisible, not only because we have not seen God but because we *cannot* see God. When God reveals himself to us, therefore, we have somehow to be enabled to "hear sounds" that our "ears" are unfit to perceive. Another analogy might illustrate this point. A scientist who had been studying elephants for decades at one point decided to listen to the elephants' sounds with the help of an ultrasonic device, and for the first time she realized that she had never heard their real language before. She found out, for instance, that infrasounds enable elephants to hear each other even several miles away. We can say that the "device," so to speak, that allows us to hear the infrasound of divine revelation is none other than the Trinity.[37] I can hear the Father only if the Son reveals him to me. I can hear the Son's revelation of the Father only as the Holy Spirit enables me to perceive it. The act of hearing is possible only if I am introduced into the life of the Trinity and only if the listening to the Word becomes conversion. I can welcome the Father's revelation only as I let myself be reconciled with him by Christ through the Holy Spirit.[38]

37. Karl Barth, *Church Dogmatics* I/1, ed. G. W. Bromiley, trans. Harold Knight (London: T&T Clark, 1936), 119. (Henceforth, Barth, CD I/1.)

38. Barth, CD I/1, 119.

This means that the word of God is God speaking to me (*Dei loquentis persona*) and that this never becomes something I can take for granted, a message I have heard once for all or that I can encapsulate in propositions valid once for all. Word means communication based on communion: the communication happens only insofar and as long as the relationship is there. It is an unceasing action, a repeated event: "This third form of the Word of God [the Word of God as *event*] needs to be stressed because *Bible* and *proclamation* are not the Word of God but must constantly *become* the Word of God: the *Bible* by attesting (being a witness, pointing away from itself) revelation; *proclamation* by repeating the Bible as witness to revelation."[39]

In this context, the theological significance of Barth's description of monasticism-as-action becomes clearer. Monastic life is a ministry to God, preserves its exemplary role, and can generate communities gathered and sustained by God's call only insofar as it remains *an action*, an *event*. Talking about monasticism as a "state of perfection," as order, can lead us to forget that it owes its origin and its existence solely and incessantly to the event of revelation and reconciliation. A monastic tradition too reliant on forms, customs, rules, and practices can become a hindrance to monasticism-as-action. Drawing inspiration from one of Barth's most eloquent images, we can compare monasticism-as-action to the giant billboards overlooking Times Square in New York: unless electricity passes through them, they remain indistinguishable from the darkness of the night.[40]

In the direction of the resurrection

Another essential feature of this monasticism-as-action and of its dependence on the word of God is that the event of revelation

39. Barth, CD I/1, 117.
40. Barth, CD IV/1, 619. Also: "The Christian simply is a reflector such as we have on our roads, with no intrinsic power of illumination" (614).

not only gives life to a Christian person, to the church, and therefore to a monastic community—it also gives them a distinctive form and a characteristic organizing dynamic. This is what Barth calls "direction." The forms that monasticism-as-action has taken throughout history have been shaped by the "direction" and the "consistent orientation" Christ's resurrection conveys to human existence.[41] They are an expression of what has been called the "self-organizing power of the Gospel."[42]

Barth attributes the historical and theological predominance of the right sequence between faith and works in monastic tradition precisely to the acknowledgement of the resurrection as "direction."[43] When we step into a river, we feel the might of its current, and if we do not resist it, we are effortlessly carried downstream. Barth describes the resurrection as a stream and its direction is the shape it gives to monastic life as "discipleship, sanctification, concretion, brotherhood and love."[44] These are the forms monasticism must take if the word of God truly becomes event, action in its midst: "The Resurrection, in the Holy Spirit, is a *direction* which becomes the principle of sanctification, effects the upbuilding of the community, in the eventuation of Christian love."[45]

Of course, the exemplary or "representational" role of this monasticism-as-action is provisional,[46] fragmentary, and incomplete.[47] Although provisional, however, it is genuine and even invincible because, like the church, a monastic community is not only "activated," so to speak, by God's words, but is also "continually

---

41. Barth, CD IV/2, 15.

42. Cf. John Webster, "The Self-organizing Power of the Gospel of Christ: Episcopacy and Community Formation," in *Word and Church: Essays in Christian Dogmatics* (Edinburgh: T&T Clark, 2001), 191–210.

43. Barth, CD IV/2, 18.

44. Barth, CD IV/2, 18.

45. Barth, CD IV/1, 614.

46. Barth, CD IV/1, 620.

47. Barth, CD IV/1, 621.

fitted" or "equipped" for this action by it,[48] according to a passage from Paul's letter to the Ephesians that Barth often quotes in this context: "He gave some as apostles, others as prophets, others as evangelists, others as pastors and teachers, to equip the holy ones for the work of ministry, for building up the body of Christ, until we all attain to the unity of faith and knowledge of the Son of God, to mature manhood, to the extent of the full stature of Christ" (Eph 4:11-14).

We should visualize this being equipped as the movement of a whirlwind that not only moves forward but also gathers everything in its course. The impetus of the resurrection not only draws us toward the Father, it also makes us brothers and sisters. Again here Barth quotes Ephesians: "Through him the whole structure is held together and grows into a temple sacred in the Lord" (Eph 2:21). This upbuilding consists in the mutual adaptation, reciprocal dependence, and support that is *agape*.[49] Within the community, this upbuilding takes the form of reciprocal edification and shared consolation, as we find in 1 Corinthians: "one who prophesies does speak to human beings, for their building up, encouragement, and solace" (1 Cor 14:3). The church is the event of this upbuilding as a community.[50] This direction translates into a distinctive Christian ethos: everything Christians do is to be judged by whether it serves this integration, this edification, this upbuilding.[51]

No gradations of calling

In this description of what allows monasticism to be an *action* corresponding to the *direction* of the word of God, Barth takes issue with any interpretation that drives a wedge between monastic vocation and the call addressed to all Christians. It was understandable, he says, that in the course of history "distinctions had

48. Barth, CD IV/1, 623.
49. Barth, CD IV/1, 636.
50. Barth, CD IV/1, 641.
51. Barth, CD IV/1, 637.

to be drawn between the vigilant and active on the one side [that is, monks and nuns] and the sleepy and indolent on the other." These descriptions, however, "ought not to have been interpreted as distinctions between perfect and imperfect, or gradations of calling."[52] This trend had such an influence in the history of the church that until recent times very few would have applied the term *vocation* to those who come to faith and ask to be baptized. This term was reserved to the call to embrace any form of ordained or charismatic ministry in the church.

For Barth this is not just a philological nicety; rather, it betrays a deeper theological misunderstanding that endangers the integrity of both Christian life and monastic ministry. He starts by observing that the main term the New Testament uses to refer to the believer is not *Christian* but *kletos*, meaning "one who is called."[53] The use of the words *qahal* ("convocation") in the Old Testament and of *ekklesia* (from *enkaleo*, "to call out of ") in the New Testament to designate the community of believers conveys exactly the same idea: the assembly comes to existence only because it is summoned and gathered by the call of the word of God. The structural relation to the word of God in Christian life means that "vocation" or "call" is what makes us Christians. This core truth of our faith lost most of its power in the context of institutional Christianity where infant baptism and sociological constraints obscured the fact that nobody is a Christian unless he actually, constantly, personally, and consciously responds to God's calling—not only initially, but every day.

Reclaiming this biblical understanding of call or "vocation" corresponds with Barth's theology of the word of God as the living presence of Christ as prophet in the midst of his church and with the corresponding ministry of *witnessing* entrusted to all Christians.

---

52. Barth, CD IV/2, 15.

53. Karl Barth, *Church Dogmatics* IV/3.2, ed. G. W. Bromiley, trans. Harold Knight (London: T&T Clark, 1957), 525. (Henceforth, Barth, CD IV/3.2.)

Resisting individualism

Whiffs of nineteenth-century individualism are sometimes still in the air in monastic circles. There are monks who are models of monastic discipline, spend long hours in prayer, and zealously fulfil the tasks entrusted to them, while disliking interactions and living at the edge of the community. This attitude embodies a distinctive stream of spirituality promoted by romantic ascetical pamphlets based on an individualistic and voluntarist understanding of redemption. These writings describe the monastic calling as a flight from the world to pursue one's own salvation and are permeated by a shocking anthropological pessimism, reflected, for example, in Thomas à Kempis's comment, "As often as I have been among men, I have returned less a man."[54] Most monastic hagiography, especially since the Counter-Reformation, adopts this soteriological model and favors the implausible image of a monk spending his time kneeling in a cave and looking at a crucifix, with a skull as his only furniture.

In his dealings with unsatisfactory versions of Christian vocation, Barth addresses this form of soteriological individualism in the context of his criticism of the "*pro me*" theme so familiar to Protestant homiletic and spirituality. Christian vocation is not first of all a call to be saved and "to enjoy the benefits of salvation."[55] We might think that nothing is "more relevant than that which in supreme and ultimate matters concerns me"[56] and that a Christian should "be supremely interested in the goal of vocation from the standpoint of its personal or 'existential' relevance to himself."[57] Too much, however, in this approach "would depend upon my strong or feeble assurance of salvation."[58] This "would sanction

54. Thomas à Kempis, *The Imitation of Christ*, trans. William Benham (London: Routledge, 1900), 20.
55. Barth, CD IV/3.2, 561.
56. Barth, CD IV/3.2, 563.
57. Barth, CD IV/3.2, 566.
58. Barth, CD IV/3.2, 565.

and cultivate an egocentricity which is only too human for all its sanctity."[59] And anyway, Barth adds, even from the historical point of view, spiritual movements which stressed the "*pro me*" were not at all quiet! "They could not refrain from talking about these things"[60] and indeed "gave real impulse to evangelical mission."[61]

A healthy theological answer to these individualistic approaches to Christian vocation is that the "goal of vocation is to be *in Christ*, and Christ cannot simply be the means to something else."[62] The Gospels start with Jesus' call to his disciples to follow him. This call expresses the essence of vocation, of salvation, of the church, and of the life to come: to become Christians is to be with Christ. Eternal life will consist in being with Christ, at least in Paul's most concise description of it: "Thus we shall always be with the Lord" (1 Thess 4:17); "That Christ should live in the Christian is the goal of his vocation"[63]; and "the principle which controls Christian existence consists in the *community of action* with him."[64]

The use of the word *action* in this last sentence echoes the description of monasticism-as-action that is guiding our reflection. Being with Christ "activates" us to fellowship with each other. However, Barth also makes clear that "fellowship of life finds realization as a *differentiated* fellowship of action."[65] The fact that there is no gradation of calling in Christianity does not mean that there is no *differentiation* with regards to *action* and therefore that there are no specific ways of answering this same call, one of which is the monastic ministry. The call, however, is the same for all because there is no higher or more perfect or more effective call than the one the living word addresses to all people.

59. Barth, CD IV/3.2, 567.
60. Barth, CD IV/3.2, 568.
61. Barth, CD IV/3.2, 569.
62. Barth, CD IV/3.2, 595.
63. Barth, CD IV/3.2, 594.
64. Barth, CD IV/3.2, 597.
65. Barth, CD IV/3.2, 598.

The monastic task

Precisely because to be called is to be in Christ and because Christ's identity cannot be separated from his mission, monastic vocation, too, is essentially to be given a task. Barth observes that all biblical accounts of vocations have one thing in common: "that to be called means to be given a task"[66] and "the essence of their vocation is that God makes them his witnesses."[67] Christian existence is first of all determined by "a commission, a function to be exercised between God and other people, between God and the world."[68]

Ultimately, therefore, Christian vocation has to do with the fact that Christ is the Word of God and that to be with him is to echo this Word by the direction it impresses on one's life, both individually and as a community. One of Barth's ways of conveying the same idea is to say that "Christ calls the Christians so that we may speak of their cooperation in his prophetic work. This then, the divine Word, is the *telos* and meaning of their service."[69]

The essence of a reconfiguring of monastic vocation as the action summoned, shaped, and sustained by the Word of God, or by Christ as Prophet (another way of saying the same thing), is therefore that it has to give witness to God's action of revelation and reconciliation. "In the New Testament Christ himself is the witness. But the self-witness of Jesus not only calls the Christian to be his witness but appoints and makes him such."[70] Christians, monks, nuns can do this only as human beings and therefore within the limits represented by their sinful existence and its possibilities. The ministry of monastic life is indeed exemplary for the church, but just like any other form of witness to Christ, it "cannot be more or other than a human indication and attestation of the Word of God—if Christ did not bear witness to himself, of what

66. Barth, CD IV/3.2, 573.
67. Barth, CD IV/3.2, 575.
68. Barth, CD IV/3.2, 592.
69. Barth, CD IV/3.2, 607.
70. Barth, CD IV/3.2, 614.

avail would be even the best witness with which the Christian can serve him?"[71]

Solidarity with nonbelievers

This point leads us to a final aspect of monastic calling, ministry, and witness in relation to the word of God that we should not overlook. Monks and nuns are supposed to be believers who take their Christian vocation seriously; the call is indeed the same for all Christians. Yet monasticism really brings a difference to this call through what Barth calls "a teleological concretion of the Christian status," by which he means "a practical and regulated brotherhood . . . in the service of concrete and total love."[72] One aspect of this total love, this solidarity, is that it reaches out not only to other Christians but to all people, irrespective of their religion or non-religion, and therefore to nonbelievers too. With regard to this last category, monasticism-as-action—that is, a monasticism that truly keeps listening to the word of God—paradoxically leads to an even greater solidarity with people who struggle with the nonevidence of God.

The most intriguing feature of Barth's approach to revelation is precisely the fact that God does not cease to be invisible, unknowable, *in* his revelation. If revelation and the church exist only as events, if monasticism can be truthful only as action, it is because our unbelief, our sloth, our resistance to God constantly need to be overcome by God's grace. A plane flies not because it is dispensed from the law of gravity, but only thanks to its powerful engines and only as long as it is propelled by them. If this thrust stops, the plane immediately crashes. If monasticism ceases to be "action," it ceases to be Christian.

With relation to this aspect, monasticism is helped by what Barth calls the *secularity* of the word of God. He explains that we

71. Barth, CD IV/3.2, 609.
72. Barth, CD IV/2, 18.

do not have the word of God otherwise than in the mystery of its secularity—that is, of a "double indirectness."[73] It reaches us under the form of a creaturely reality that also is a fallen reality,[74] a reality that contradicts God. Scripture, preaching, Christian witness, the ministry, and the exemplary role of monastic communities are not so much *that through which* God reveals himself, but *that in spite of which* God miraculously manages to make himself known.[75] This inevitable opacity of all created realities, even those God uses to reveal himself, is what Karl Barth calls the "secularity" of the word of God. God has chosen to reveal himself through a medium that contradicts him. This secularity is not accidental or provisional, but an inalienable attribute of the word of God.[76] This explains why revelation is an event, an action. The opacity, the resistance of created and fallen realities to revelation, is never overcome once for all. Only the active presence of the risen Christ, who keeps speaking his word, and the work of the Holy Spirit in our hearts enable us to receive it. Secularity is overcome as a result of an *act*, that is never once for all.[77] To ignore or try to evade this secularity, says Barth, is to evade Christ who in his incarnation has entered into this secularity.[78]

Only relying on God's mercy

A key corollary of the secularity of the word of God for monks and nuns, therefore, is that their lives, their liturgies, their reading of Scripture (their *lectio divina*), their community life, their ministry, and their witness never lose a level of imperviousness to God's grace and of ambiguity. Their faith remains a constant challenge for

73. Barth, CD I/1, 165.
74. Barth, CD I/1, 166.
75. Barth, CD I/1, 166.
76. Barth, CD I/1, 168.
77. Barth, CD I/1, 171.
78. Barth, CD I/1, 168.

them as for any other Christian. "A Christian does not see more than a non-Christian, but he trusts [Christ] and follows him in darkness."[79] This explains the suspicion Barth (and most of the Protestant tradition) feels against some forms of mysticism. In his understanding, "*mysticism* regards the secularity of Bible and of Christ as mere symbols which become dispensable once their content has been revealed; *faith*, on the contrary, immediately returns to the Bible and Christ in their secularity" and keeps relying on God's faithfulness alone.[80]

Far from impairing the ministry of monasticism-as-action, this awareness enhances the exemplary role of monasticism. Whoever has lived in a monastery as a monk or a nun long enough or has benefited as a lay person from the proximity to the life of a monastic community knows that the infallible hallmark of a spirituality authentically shaped by an effective listening of the word of God is the key Benedictine value of humility.

Thus, for example, a superficial reader of chapter four of Benedict's Rule, on "the tools for good works," could be led to think that monastic life is all about systematic focusing on good practices. It is striking, however, that this list of seventy-two exhortations should end with a recommendation that prevents any possible temptation of self-reliance or any illusion that Christian life and witness might consist in becoming models of perfection. The last of these exhortations is to "never lose hope in God's mercy" (RB 4.74), which means that monasticism-as-action must never lose sight of the uncertainty and ambiguity of human endeavors and of the constant opacity of any form of human witness.

Therefore, the exemplary role of monasticism, the essential feature of Christian life monasticism-as-action gives witness to, is the infallible power of God's grace and mercy in the midst of an ever-increasing awareness of human opposition to it. It is precisely this tension, this paradox, that explains, for Barth, the fruitfulness

79. Barth, CD I/1, 170.
80. Barth, CD I/1, 178.

of monasticism and its extraordinary resilience in spite of all its shortcomings. This is how monasticism contributes to the life of the church: "More that this human witness is not demanded of [it]. But the service of this human witness"[81] is necessary in a church and in a world that more than ever needs to learn the power of relying on God's mercy alone.

81. Barth, CD IV/3.2, 609.

CHAPTER X

Listening

Novice and senior monk are "obeying" one another if
they are attending with discernment to one another,
and the habits that shape their lives are habits of
listening, attention and the willingness to take
seriously the perspective of the other, the stranger.

Rowan Williams[1]

At the structural center of the prologue of the Rule of Benedict, we find this sentence: "Clothed then with faith and the performance of good works, let us set out on this way, with the Gospel for our guide, that we may deserve to see him 'who has called us to his kingdom'" (RB Prol. 21, citing 1 Thess 2:12). The Rule is not self-referential. To show monastics the way to follow, Benedict points not to his own wisdom, but *"per ducatum Evangelii"*—that is, to the guidance of the Gospel.

The Rule's deepest meaning is found in the context of a path of conversion that only the word of God can sustain and renew. Conversion, in fact, does not consist in adhering to the articles of a creed or to moral principles. These (which theology calls the "objective content of faith") are a consequence of adhering to God in Christ and in the Spirit (the so-called "formal principle of

1. Williams, *The Way of St Benedict*, 35.

faith"), as the Gospels clearly show us. The meaning of conversion to Jesus for his disciples is illustrated by the story of the call of the first disciples. Jesus doesn't begin by asking them to profess a creed or to observe a set of moral rules; he invites them to follow him, to dwell with him: "From that time on, Jesus began to preach and say, 'Repent, for the kingdom of heaven is at hand.' As he was walking by the Sea of Galilee, he saw two brothers, Simon who is called Peter, and his brother Andrew, casting a net into the sea; they were fishermen. He said to them, 'Come after me, and I will make you fishers of men'" (Matt 4:17-19).

Conversion is a movement of dwelling in ever-deeper unity with Christ. It is not a path of progressive moral improvement, but a God-centered journey. The Rule speaks of a path of *dilatatio cordis*, a widening of the heart, and the only things that widens the heart are faith, hope, and love: "As we progress in this way of life and in faith, we shall run on the path of God's commandments, our hearts overflowing with the inexpressible delights of love" (RB Prol. 49). Precisely because only the word of God can arouse and nourish conversion, faith, love, and hope, the Rule simply aspires to become the Word's instrument, constantly referring to it. And so the prologue begins with the exhortation to listen to "the master's instructions" and the "advice from a father who loves you" (RB Prol. 1), and it ends by specifying that the *magisterium* and the *doctrina* that must be taught are those of God: we must "never [swerve] from [God's] instructions, then, but faithfully [observe] his teaching" (RB Prol. 50).

A whole range of actions then listed in the prologue have God's Word as their subject. The Word shakes us awake every morning: "Let us get up then, at long last, for the Scriptures rouse us when they say: 'It is high time for us to arise from sleep'" (RB Prol. 8; cf. Rom 13:11). And it admonishes us: "Let us open our eyes to the light that comes from God, and our ears to the voice from heaven that every day calls out" (RB Prol. 9). The prologue gathers scriptural quotations not simply to support the master's instructions, but to let God, through his word, invite us, seek us out, and teach us: "You that have ears to hear, listen. . . . I will teach you the fear of the Lord. . . . Is there anyone here who yearns for life? . . . Let peace be your quest and aim" (RB Prol. 11, 12, 15, 17, quoting Rev 2:7; Ps 33[34]:12, 13, 15). In this way, the decisive questions are asked by God and the promises made in the Rule are reliable because God guarantees them: "Once you have done this, my eyes will be upon you and my ears will listen to your prayers; and even before you ask me, I will say to you: Here I am" (RB Prol. 18, quoting Isa 58:9). The master concludes by asking: "What, dear brothers, is more delightful than this voice of the Lord calling to us?" (RB Prol. 19).

But the primacy of the Word in monastic life has a still deeper theological and spiritual foundation. In Christianity, a rule, a code of conduct, even a sapiential exhortation (which is the literary genre to which the Rule's prologue belongs) do not have value in themselves, independently, whatever the author's moral authority may be. If a rule, exhortation, law, or the simple fact of saying or knowing what to do was enough to save us, there would have been no need for God to become incarnate in Christ and, above all, to die on the cross. From the beginning, Christianity has been tempted to seek its own security in the Law instead of faith. Even today, Paul continues to insistently put to us the same questions he poses to the Galatians of his own day: "Does, then, the one who supplies the Spirit to you and works mighty deeds among you do so from works of the law or from faith in what you heard?" (Gal 3:5). Like the Galatians, we are constantly "so stupid" that "after beginning with the Spirit," we "[end] with the flesh" (Gal 3:3)—that is, with the preference for justice at the low price of conformity and of rules instead of allowing ourselves to be provoked by Jesus' constant challenge, his "but I tell you." We prefer the justice "of the scribes and Pharisees" (Matt 5:20), believing that it's enough to follow certain practices, forms, and rules, instead of constantly following Jesus, seeking no other security than to know that we are with him. We are justified, not just initially, but continuously, not by conforming to a rule, but by listening to the word of faith, the Word that alone has the power to arouse faith, to awaken it, and to continually reawaken it, because *fides ex auditu*, "faith comes from what is heard" (Rom 10:17).

Holding fast

For this reason, among the first statements of Benedict's Rule is not an injunction but an invitation to become aware of a fact: daily we are exposed to a call, to an appeal. It is enough for us to open our eyes to realize that there is a voice that continually— *now, today*—calls us and alerts us: "If you hear his voice today, do not harden your hearts" (RB Prol. 10, citing Ps 94:8). All day, especially in monastic life, we are exposed to an outpouring of God's word through the celebration of the liturgy. But listening to it cannot be merely passive. The Word must be welcomed, internalized, meditated upon, allowed to settle in one's heart: *inclina aurem cordis tui*, "attend with the ear of your heart" (RB Prol. 1). This "attending" or "inclining" suggests the movement necessary to listen better.

In this sense, there is a parallel between the Rule and the book of Psalms. Both declare from the beginning that the nature of our life depends on our relationship with the Word: "Blessed is the man who does not walk / in the counsel of the wicked. / Nor stand in the way of sinners, / nor sit in company with scoffers. / Rather, the law of the LORD is his joy; / and on his law he meditates day and night" (Ps 1:1-2).

Happiness, joy, self-fulfillment, the blossoming of all one's gifts, a full life that is worth living—this is the meaning of the adjective *blessed* that begins this sentence. This kind of blessedness is the result of one's relationship to the Word (*law* in this passage means "word of God"), the care with which we listen to it, the attention we give it. It is interesting that this psalm is not a prayer of thanks or supplication or trust; rather, it is simply the affirmation of a fact, that the success of our lives depends on where we decide to sink our roots. If our roots draw from the living water of the

Word, then we are "like a tree / planted near streams of water / that yields its fruit in season; / Its leaves never wither; / whatever he does prospers. / . . . Because the LORD knows the way of the just" (Ps 1:3, 6).

This perspective is typical of the theology of the Deuteronomist, insisting that the fundamental decision that determines the course of one's existence is to love God and to walk in God's ways: "See, I have today set before you life and good, death and evil. If you obey the commandments of the LORD, your God, which I am giving you today, loving the LORD, your God, and walking in his ways, and keeping his commandments, statutes and ordinances, you will live and grow numerous, and the LORD, your God, will bless you in the land you are entering to possess. . . . Choose life, then, that you and your descendants may live, by loving the LORD, your God, obeying his voice, and holding fast to him" (Deut 30:15-16, 19-20).

The whole secret of Christian life is in this "holding fast to him"—in all circumstances, whatever our hearts might reproach us, and against every temptation to discouragement—because "God is greater than our hearts" (1 John 3:20). The secret of *living*, then, is to choose to remain united to the Lord by listening to his word, while being "wicked" means allowing oneself to be carried along by the force of inertia, by the current, by imitating what we see around us, by walking "in the counsel of the wicked," standing "in the way of sinners," or sitting "in company with scoffers" (Ps 1:1). We hope to hide ourselves among this "company," but they are blown away "like chaff driven by the wind" (Ps 1:4), because they are not true communities, but are held together by nothing more than opportunism, self-interest, or fear. The "just," on the other hand—that is, those who made the choice to listen to the Word—are welcomed into "the assembly of the just" (Ps 1:5), the *qahal YHWH*. This assembly is the community established on the call of God. Its unity is founded on the action and the fidelity of God, and for this reason it is a stable dwelling that reaches its fulfillment in the communion of saints for eternity.

Delighting and meditating

Even though this psalm speaks of the *just* and the *wicked*, the distinction is not primarily a *moral* one; it doesn't depend on acting, on doing, but rather on *what we find pleasure in* and *meditating on*: "the law of the LORD is [the blessed one's] joy; / and on his law he meditates day and night" (Ps 1:2). Here, too, the reference to "the law" means the word of God as a whole—not an external, restrictive imposition that binds one's freedom, but the set of words and testimonies that the Holy Spirit uses to instruct us, console us, guide us, and enlighten us, and which we act upon only if we have internalized it, only if it we love it. Paraphrasing the psalms that speak of love for the law, we might say this: "The word of the LORD is perfect, refreshing the soul. The word of the LORD is trustworthy, giving wisdom to the simple. The word of the LORD is right, rejoicing the heart. The word of the LORD is clear, enlightening the eye" (cf. Ps 19:8-9, but also all of Ps 119).

We are invited to unify our whole life through finding pleasure and joy in the assiduous meditation on the word of God. The verb *to meditate* means to murmur, to whisper: "The mouth of the righteous utters wisdom; / his tongue speaks what is right. / God's teaching is in his heart" (Ps 37:30-31). The words in the original Hebrew suggest the cooing of a dove, *meditabor ut columba*: "Like a swallow I chirp; / I moan like a dove" (Isa 38:14). It is not primarily a mental meditation, but a repetition, a sort of chewing that slowly releases all the flavors. But the result of this meditation is not just taste but nourishment. It produces fruit; it is fecund; it gives life. Whoever devotes himself to it is "like a tree planted beside the waters / that stretches out its roots to the stream: / It does not fear heat when it comes, / its leaves stay green; / In the year of drought it shows no distress, / but still produces fruit" (cf. Jer 17:8). "The just shall flourish like the palm tree, / shall grow like a cedar of Lebanon" (Ps 92:13).

The last verse of Psalm 1 summarizes the endpoint of this journey: "The LORD knows the way of the just, / but the way of the wicked leads to ruin" (Ps 1:6). The asymmetry is intentional.

The first half of the sentence has as its subject "the LORD" and as its complement "the way"; but in the second half, "the way" is the subject. This expresses a profound theological truth: the positive outcome of a life is the result of the Lord's action. Its failure is not caused or desired or even permitted by the Lord, nor is it a punishment; rather, it comes from having opted for a non-choice, from having surrendered to the force of inertia, from letting oneself be carried away by the group ("the wicked," "sinners," "scoffers").

Also interesting is the verb that expresses the Lord's action in our lives: *knows*. "The LORD *knows* the days of the blameless" (Ps 37:18); "I will rejoice and be glad in your mercy, / once you have seen my misery, / and *gotten to know* the distress of my soul" (Ps 31:8). The psalmist often confesses that the Lord "*knows* the secrets of the heart" (Ps 44:22). The Lord is interested in us, in our lives, in each of our actions. Nothing we do is too ordinary, too trivial for the Father: "LORD, you have probed me, you *know* me: / you *know* when I sit and stand; / you understand my thoughts from afar. / You sift through my travels and my rest; / with all my ways you are familiar" (Ps 139:1-3).

The believers constantly discover how the Lord accompanies them and assists them on their journey through the great desert: "It is now forty years that the LORD, your God, has been with you, and you have lacked nothing" (Deut 2:7). All of human existence unfolds under the sign of the Lord's care and love: "Before I formed you in the womb I knew you" (Jer 1:5).

In this contrast between the attitude of the just and that of the wicked toward the Word, we find the results of the Gospel parable of the sower. Those whose hearts are a favorable soil for the Word—listening to it, meditating upon it, and putting it into practice—bear fruit: "Those sown on rich soil are the ones who hear the word and accept it and bear fruit thirty and sixty and a hundredfold" (Mark 4:20). But for those in whom the Word cannot put down roots or who are among the brambles, the Word is immediately neutralized, dried up, suffocated, and unable to act (cf. Mark 4:15-19).

A community created by the Word

What is the fruit of the Word? What harvest does this welcoming of the Word produce in individuals and in communities? One of the most interesting answers to this question is offered in narrative form by both Luke and Paul in their story of the Thessalonian community. It is interesting to reread the account of the evangelization of this community in the book of the Acts of the Apostles (written by Luke) alongside the one Paul offers in his first letter to this same community.

In Acts, we read that Paul, arriving in Thessalonica, "following his usual custom," went for three Saturdays in a row to the synagogue to proclaim the good news he bore. Luke describes the content of his message, writing that Paul "entered into discussions with [the Jews] from the scriptures, expounding and demonstrating that the Messiah had to suffer and rise from the dead, and that 'This is the Messiah, Jesus, whom I proclaim to you'" (Acts 17:2-3). There were a few conversions among the Jews and some others among the Greeks, but soon a violent persecution was unleashed, and Paul had to flee the city quickly (Acts 17:4-10). As a result, the Christians of Thessalonica received only an initial evangelization. There was only enough time for them to receive the core of the Christian proclamation (the *kerygma*), that Christ is the key to interpreting the Scriptures (by which, at that time, was meant only what we now call the Old Testament). These Christians may have received baptism, but there was no time for anything else—Paul wasn't able to leave any minister behind and so had to abandon them or, rather, left them equipped with nothing else than the ability to experience the living and effective presence of the risen Christ through his Word by his Spirit.

Paul's first letter to the Thessalonians takes up the story where Acts leaves off, and Paul tells it in the first person. We see him in the grip of great anxiety about this community; with a barely begun evangelization and the immediate outbreak of violent persecution, he feared that the faith of the Thessalonians would be wiped out.[2] He tried several times to return, but this proved impossible.[3] When he "could bear it no longer," he decided to send to Thessalonica "Timothy, our brother and co-worker for God in the gospel of Christ, to strengthen and encourage you in your faith, so that no one be disturbed in these afflictions" (1 Thess 3:1-2). Considering these concerns, Paul was surprised when Timothy returned from Thessalonica with unexpected news: "Just now Timothy has returned to us from you, bringing us the good news of your faith and love, and that you always think kindly of us and long to see us as we long to see you" (1 Thess 3:6). We mustn't miss the reason for Paul's relief: "We have been reassured about you, brothers . . . through your faith" and because "you stand firm in the Lord" (cf. 1 Thess 3:7-8). Another passage provides further detail: "We give thanks to God always for all of you, remembering you in our prayers, unceasingly calling to mind your work of *faith* and labor of *love* and endurance in *hope* of our Lord Jesus Christ, before our God and Father" (1 Thess 1:2-3, emphasis added).

Inexplicably, despite the fragility of the community's new faith and the wave of persecution, not only did the young and small community survive, but faith, hope, and charity flourished there, as did the key New Testament virtue of *hypomoné* (perseverance or endurance). And these neophytes not only held onto their faith; they also became evangelizers and a model for other communities.[4] What explains such a result? How was this possible? What allowed this community to develop so rapidly and such a

2. 1 Thess 3:5: "When I too could bear it no longer, I sent to learn about your faith, for fear that somehow the tempter had put you to the test and our toil might come to nothing."

3. 1 Thess 2:18: "We decided to go to you—I, Paul, not only once but more than once—yet Satan thwarted us."

4. 1 Thess 1:7-8: "You became a model for all the believers in Macedonia and in Achaia. For from you the word of the Lord has sounded forth not only in Macedonia and in Achaia, but in every place your faith in God has gone forth, so that we have no need to say anything."

missionary spirit to thrive so abundantly? Paul himself provides an answer to this question: "For this reason we thank God continually because, when you received the word of God, which you heard from us, you accepted it not as a human word, but as it truly is, the word of God, which is indeed at work in you who believe" (1 Thess 2:13). The answer is that they thrived because they had read Scripture in such way as to perceive the voice and follow the guidance of the living God.

Paul himself at times lacked faith. He was like many other pastors and ministers in the history of the church who, as much as they believed in Jesus' promises and in his presence through the Holy Spirit, continued to act as if everything depended on them, as if the success of their evangelizing work were merely the result of human strategies. Only in the face of evidence was Paul able to recognize that the word of God was indeed active, that it truly works in believers when it is received "as it truly is, the word of God" (1 Thess 2:13), when it is received "with joy from the holy Spirit" (1 Thess 1:6). The Word is active because it converts those who receive it to the "living and true" God: "They themselves openly declare about us what sort of reception we had among you, and how you turned to God from idols to serve the living and true God" (1 Thess 1:9).

The message of Acts and 1 Thessalonians therefore is clear: it is the word of God that builds the community. The church, as a whole and in each of its local communities, is a *creatura verbi* ("creature of the Word"); it is the result of the constant, creative, life-giving, and regenerating action of the Word. Every Christian community continues to exist only to the extent that it constantly allows itself to be recreated, called together, shaped, consoled, guided, and instructed by the Word proclaimed, meditated upon, welcomed, and lived within. The Word is not an instrument to which we give life by our proclamation or meditation. If we are able to proclaim it, meditate on it, welcome it, and live it, it is because it is "living and effective, sharper than any two-edged sword, penetrating even between soul and spirit, joints and marrow, and able to discern reflections and thoughts of the heart" (Heb 4:12).

Seeking God as Father

It is no surprise, then, that the first word of Benedict's Rule is an invitation to listen: "Listen carefully, my son, to the master's instructions, and attend to them with the ear of your heart. This is advice from a father who loves you; welcome it, and faithfully put it into practice. The labor of obedience will bring you back to him from whom you had drifted through the sloth of disobedience" (RB Prol. 1-2).

That the person we should listen to is "the master" does not change anything, because this master can exercise his leadership role only to the extent that he echoes the word of God: "The abbot must never teach or decree or command anything that would deviate from the Lord's instructions. On the contrary, everything he teaches and commands should, like the leaven of divine justice, permeate the minds of his disciples" (RB 2.4). And significantly, this invitation is addressed to a "son/daughter" and it can be addressed *only* to a *son* or *daughter*—that is, to *someone who accepts the word of God with the trust and freedom of a child*. The first and fundamental definition of the monastic is precisely this—the monastic is, in his or her relationship with God, a son or daughter and knows God as Father.

The word *son/daughter* evokes first of all the awareness of a relationship of dependence: the Father gave me life; he continues to give it to me every day; I receive it constantly from the One in whom "we live and move and have our being" (cf. Acts 17:28). Consequently, *son/daughter* evokes not just the reality of having received a gift, but also the giver and therefore gratitude. The spiritual tradition has often opposed *filial gratitude* to two other ways of relating to God: as *servant* and as *merchant*. We are in a *servile* relationship with God when we act out of fear or need, and we are in a *mercantile* relationship when we obey out of self-interest, using our obedience as a bargaining chip to get something in return. The son or daughter is the one who acts freely and out of love.

Not just officials

We should note that today, servile and mercantile logic have lost much of the power they once had to dilute the life of faith. True, modern and post-modern critiques of faith and a greater aware- ness of the psychological mechanisms of the unconscious have perhaps created more obstacles to faith in our day; at the same time, however, they have had the unexpectedly positive effect of making faith more clearly a free choice. The tangle of social and cultural factors that affected religiosity in the past, and that made the choice for faith less free and personal, have lost much of their coercive effect.

But the idolatry that lives in the heart of the human person is never short of resources; it is a hydra that is not defeated simply by cutting off its heads because it grows new ones. It is a fight that is never fully won. It can be fought only by the power of the Word that, as mentioned above, penetrates "even between soul and spirit, joints and marrow, and discerns reflections and thoughts of the heart" (Heb 4:12).

A cataloguing of the most common perversions of the relation- ship with God in our day would have to start with *the logic of of- ficials*. For those who have received the sacrament of holy orders or those in religious life, ministry can become an activity or a job like any other. Working for the church can replace one's personal, filial relationship with the Lord. We put ourselves in good standing by carrying out tasks, fulfilling our duties, dispensing the sacraments, organizing the activities normally associated with pastoral care, all along ignoring a growing sense of inner emptiness. One becomes an impassive official of an institution, forgetting that the meaning of our mission as well as our Christian identity rests entirely on a true and living relationship with the Father. Those who perform this kind of service in the church but lack a grounding in a filial relationship with the Father are like a mill whose blades turn, whose millstones rotate, but which does not receive grain and so just moves air.

Frivolousness

Another problem, common in seminaries and houses of formation, is *frivolousness*. This is a kind of metamorphosis of vanity that renounces interest in fashion or worldly charms but embraces an almost fetishistic obsession for liturgical vestments, chasubles, surplices, collars, birettas, fine fabrics, the use of Latin, archaic liturgical forms, ritualism, solemnity, and so on. What is evangelical about these celebrations, often on the occasion of ordinations or otherwise presided over by bishops, with masters of ceremonies and groups of seminarians at the altar decorated in extravagant surplices with swirls of lace? It is all just a matter of "widen[ing] their phylacteries and lengthen[ing] their tassels" (Matt 23:5), transforming liturgical celebrations into tasteless fashion shows.

Such displays seem pleasant and harmless, but they are symptoms of real pathologies of the spiritual life. We see this, for example, in the fact that the most tenacious opponents of the evangelical turn to which Pope Francis has invited the church are those who refuse to renounce these tendencies. We needn't overdramatize, overstate, or even place blame here. They are symptoms, like many others, of the need we all have for continual conversion, for liberation from our idolatry in order to worship "the living and true God" (1 Thess 1:9).

Therapy

The only therapy that can unmask and neutralize all the issues that corrupt our relationship with the Father is the prayer with which Jesus taught us how to be in relationship with God: the Our Father. One of the criteria for measuring progress in the spiritual life is the authenticity, the truthfulness, and the audacity with which we pray the Our Father.

Mens nostra concordet voci nostrae—let "our minds [be] in harmony with our voices," Benedict says in his Rule (RB 19.7). This doesn't mean simply that we should be attentive to the words we say in prayer, but that we must experience as our own—ever more deeply, by grace—what the words express. The criterion for measuring progress in the spiritual life is how truly we desire the sanctification of the Father's name when we say "hallowed be thy name." And so on with the other petitions of the Our Father: how intensely do we desire the coming of the Father's kingdom, the doing of his will on earth? How well are we able to put these things before our own immediate needs? And how much do we expect, in response to these needs, to receive from the Father our daily bread, forgiveness and the ability to forgive, and the strength to resist temptations?

The true son or daughter is one who progressively allows himself or herself to be swept up into the breadth and depth of the Father's plan of salvation, embracing all of humanity and all of history. This is the meaning of one of the first sentences of the prologue of Benedict's Rule, which inserts the Christian, the monastic, the "son" or "daughter," into the heart of the mystery of salvation: "The labor of obedience will bring you back to him from whom you had drifted through the sloth of disobedience" (RB Prol. 2).

This disobedience is not only personal in nature but also one that we share collectively with all humanity. Similarly, the obedience we are asked to embrace is first of all Christ's obedience, to which we can only associate ourselves. We are all inserted into the great epic of creation, fall, and recapitulation; in Adam, we have all disobeyed, and through the obedience of the new Adam, we have all been reconciled with the Father. From the beginning of his Rule, Benedict makes clear that one does not enter monastic life in search of individual salvation, but to fully assume his or her role in the universal plan of salvation.

The son or daughter *trusts* and *listens*. Without trust there is no Christian life or, even less, monastic life. It is a trust that has to be earned on the part of those who govern and freely granted by those who obey. But its foundation is not reliance on people, but adherence to God, *faith*. Like hope and love, this faith can be aroused, preserved, and constantly reawakened only by the word of God. Only the Word converts us, not just initially, but daily. Only the Word creates and renews our hearts: "A clean heart create for me, God; / renew within me a steadfast spirit" (Ps 51:12).

The Word calls us together and builds us up, personally and as a community, inserting us ever more deeply into the universal plan of salvation. Salvation history becomes our history, Abraham becomes our father in faith, and together we await the return of Christ in glory. The Word puts on our lips a prayer that corresponds to that of the Spirit in our hearts: Our Father. The Word is the instrument par excellence of the Lord's consolation—not a passive acceptance of the inevitable or a sigh of resignation, but an understanding of the profound meaning of our lives, the beauty as well as the ugliness, the joy as well as the pain: "Blessed be the God and Father of our Lord Jesus Christ, the Father of compassion and God of all encouragement, who encourages us in our every affliction, so that we may be able to encourage those who are in any affliction with the encouragement with which we ourselves are encouraged by God" (2 Cor 1:3-4).

Prophecy

One key result of listening to the word of God in a way that is not only individual but also authentically communal is the flowering of the gift, or charism, of prophecy. We think today that this charism is the prerogative of exceptional people, forgetting that in the New Testament it was sought and cultivated as the most effective factor in building up the community.

For too long in the history of Christianity, we have thought that the fundamental elements of building and preserving the community were hierarchical and sacramental. This is a considerable impoverishment of New Testament ecclesiology, according to which the church is founded not only on the apostles (and their successors, therefore hierarchy and sacraments), but also *on prophets*. St. Paul wrote, "So then you are no longer strangers and sojourners, but you are fellow citizens with the holy ones and members of the household of God, built upon the foundation of the apostles and prophets, with Christ Jesus himself as the capstone" (Eph 2:19-20). The same idea is taken up again in the list of the charisms that Paul offers in 1 Corinthians, where mention of prophets comes immediately after apostles: "Some people God has designated in the church to be, first, apostles; second, *prophets*; third, teachers; then, mighty deeds; then, gifts of healing, assistance, administration, and varieties of tongues" (1 Cor 12:28). By limiting the church to its apostolicity, we have indirectly impoverished even the transmission of the word of God, deluding ourselves that it can be communicated effectively simply by guaranteeing its accuracy and preserving doctrinal orthodoxy.

That the church is founded on the apostles *and on prophets* means that the Word is transmitted effectively not only, nor even primarily, by the exactness of the message but also when it is communicated in a way that enables it to speak to people's hearts, to convert them. This requires a special charism, that of prophecy, that is not automatically conferred with the sacrament of order and certainly is not limited to ordained ministers.

Paul not only understands this gift as the most important one for the life of the community but urges all Christians to aspire to it: "Strive eagerly for the spiritual gifts, above all that you may prophesy" (1 Cor 14:1). The reason for this is clear when Paul describes the effects of this charism: "One who prophesies does speak to human beings, for their building up, encouragement, and solace" (1 Cor 14:3). The gift of prophecy consists in becoming instruments of the effectiveness proper to the word of God not only to instruct but, above all, to exhort and comfort—that is, to *console*, to allow everyone to grasp the profound meaning of what is proclaimed.

A Christian community—be it parochial, lay, religious, or monastic—must be constantly guided, regulated, and reinvigorated, or it will inevitably disintegrate. Despite our social instincts, we are viscerally inclined to favor self-interest over collective interest, and if this inclination is not counterbalanced by a dynamic of unity, no community is sustainable. Now, in the Christian sphere, the creation and maintenance of a community do not depend merely on a dynamic of social unity, but on an action of the Spirit that is called *edification*. Edification (*oikodomé* in Greek—that is, "the building of a house") is an important theme in 1 Corinthians. In this letter, this noun does not have the weak and moralizing sense of "providing an inspiring example" (as when talking about "edifying" behavior). Rather, it has the strong sense of "building up" or "constructing," and its result is precisely a "construction" or "building," a term that becomes synonymous with the church: "For we are God's co-workers; you are God's field, God's *building*" (1 Cor 3:9). The building up of the community is the aim of all the charisms and it is what must result from an authentic listening to the word of God by virtue of the prophetic charism: "Since you strive eagerly for spirits, seek to have an abundance of them for building up the church" (1 Cor 14:12). "Everything should be done for building up" (1 Cor 14:26).

The primacy that Paul attributes to the gift of prophecy, then, depends on the fact that this charism is the one most directly ordered to the upbuilding of the community: "Whoever speaks in a tongue builds himself up, but whoever prophesies builds up the church. Now I should like all of you to speak in tongues, but even more to prophesy. One who prophesies is greater than one who speaks in tongues, unless he interprets, so that the church may be built up" (1 Cor 14:4-5).

Prophecy, however, builds up—that is, it reaches, conquers, and converts hearts—only if it is rooted in love. This is why Paul's famous and splendid hymn to charity comes in the context of his discourse about the gifts needed for the edification of the community: "If I have the gift of prophecy and comprehend all mysteries and all knowledge; if I have all faith so as to move mountains but do not have love, I am nothing" (1 Cor 13:2). In fact, only "love builds up" (1 Cor 8:1). In order to build up, then, prophecy must be fueled by love. Behold prophecy in action: "If everyone is prophesying, and an unbeliever or uninstructed person should come in, he will be convinced by everyone and judged by everyone, and the secrets of his heart will be disclosed, and so he will fall down and worship God, declaring, 'God is really in your midst'" (1 Cor 14:24-25).

The baptized person receptive to the gift of prophecy has access to the power of the word of God to build, console, comfort, convince, judge, reveal the secrets of the heart, and thus lead to worship: "and so he will fall down and worship God" (1 Cor 14:25). This is why cultivating the gift of prophecy understood in this way is indispensable in every community. It is essential not only to the way a person listens to the Word but also to how a *community* listens. Without it, the community cannot grow or be built up.

This is why the monastic tradition has always had a clear awareness of the essential role of spiritual fathers or mothers (*starets* or *senpectae* [RB 27.2]) for a healthy community dynamic. These are people who have sought, obtained, and cultivated the charism of prophecy, and with their very lives, their word, and their spiritual accompaniment build, console, comfort, convince, judge, reveal the secrets of the heart, and so lead to worship. Anyone who has had the grace to encounter one of these figures has experienced their ability to comfort and console. Only the community capable of promoting within itself the birth and growth of this charism becomes a place in which wisdom can build her house and set her table.

CHAPTER XI

Reform

Benedict is asking what it takes to develop people who can live safely, consistently and positively together.

Rowan Williams[1]

What does it mean for monasticism to get involved in the process of "discernment, purification, and reform"[2] that Pope Francis has invited the church to embrace with decisiveness and courage? And which aspects of the reform of monasticism can, as a consequence, provide an example for the church as a whole? We will find an answer to these questions through a reading of the monastic experience in the light of Pope Francis's 2013 programmatic apostolic exhortation *Evangelii Gaudium*, a document not only of great significance for evangelization but also one of striking spiritual depth.

Making life complicated
In one of the most suggestive passages of this document, Pope Francis writes:

---

1. Williams, *The Way of St Benedict*, 28.
2. Pope Francis, apostolic exhortation *Evangelii Gaudium* (hereafter, EG) 30.

> Sometimes we are tempted to be that kind of Christian who keeps the Lord's wounds at arm's length. Yet Jesus wants us to touch human misery, to touch the suffering flesh of others. He hopes that we will stop looking for those personal or communal niches which shelter us from the maelstrom of human misfortune and instead enter into the reality of other people's lives and know the power of tenderness. Whenever we do so, our lives become wonderfully complicated and we experience intensely what it is to be a people, to be part of a people. (EG 270)

Pope Francis does not try to kid us; he knows that what he says will, if taken seriously, complicate our lives, even if it enriches them wonderfully. We must not hide the discomfort we perceive when we read the words of this apostolic exhortation. Indeed, it is meant to challenge everyone in one way or the other.

While Pope Francis is very popular in public opinion today, we must recognize that within the church he is met with an opposition that manifests itself in two forms. One is an open and sometimes angry resistance, like, for example, the one that has crystallized on some conservative fringes very active on blogs. The other is more insidious, adamant, and hidden. It does not dare to openly disagree but resists inwardly and reasons this way: we have lived well and comfortably in our roles, in our niches, in our domesticated form of the Gospel up to now—we can surely continue to do so undisturbed. Or with reasoning of this kind: it is a matter of a few years and then the pendulum will swing, and the institution's preservation instinct will prevail again, the waters will settle down, and everything will return to as before.

The first type of resistance masquerades behind a zeal for doctrinal orthodoxy, but it is often purely political. The second is strictly spiritual in nature. Realizing that we, too, are in some way accomplices in this second type of resistance shouldn't surprise us or scare us. If we discover this interior resistance even in ourselves, we needn't feel guilty, because in the end it is our habitual and inevitable resistance to the Gospel, to conversion, to the action of God. It is an unavoidable reality in our life and the lives of those around us. We know it well, and the only valid response is to humbly recognize it, repent of it, and realize that neither legalism nor arid willfulness will dissolve our hardness, our rigidity, our self-defensiveness, but only the fruits of the Spirit. As Pope Francis said in the passage quoted earlier, we are called to know the strength of God's tenderness and let it bring down our barriers, help us overcome our fears, and persuade us.

To begin with, then, we can focus on some of the most suggestive and challenging passages of *Evangelii Gaudium* and try to listen to them for a moment without filters, without fear, paying attention to what they awake in us, what effect they have on us:

> If we want to advance in the spiritual life, then, we must constantly be missionaries. The work of evangelization enriches the mind and the heart; it opens up spiritual horizons; it makes us more and more sensitive to the workings of the Holy Spirit, and it takes us beyond our limited spiritual constructs. A committed missionary knows the joy of being a spring which spills over and refreshes others. Only the person who feels happiness in seeking the good of others, in desiring their happiness, can be a missionary. This openness of the heart is a source of joy, since "it is more blessed to give than to receive" (Acts 20:35). We do not live better when we flee, hide, refuse to share, stop giving and lock ourselves up in own comforts. Such a life is nothing less than slow suicide. (EG 272)

We will see later how this call to mission applies to monastic life. For the moment, let us allow these texts to speak for themselves and let them resonate in us.

> A missionary heart is aware of these limits and makes itself "weak with the weak . . . everything for everyone" (1 Cor 9:22). It never closes itself off, never retreats into its own security, never opts for rigidity and defensiveness. It realizes that it has to grow in its own understanding of the Gospel

and in discerning the paths of the Spirit, and so it always does what good it can, even if in the process, its shoes get soiled by the mud of the street. . . .

Let us go forth, then, let us go forth to offer everyone the life of Jesus Christ. . . . I prefer a Church which is bruised, hurting and dirty because it has been out on the streets, rather than a Church which is unhealthy from being confined and from clinging to its own security. I do not want a Church concerned with being at the centre and which then ends by being caught up in a web of obsessions and procedures. If something should rightly disturb us and trouble our consciences, it is the fact that so many of our brothers and sisters are living without the strength, light and consolation born of friendship with Jesus Christ, without a community of faith to support them, without meaning and a goal in life. More than by fear of going astray, my hope is that we will be moved by the fear of remaining shut up within structures which give us a false sense of security, within rules which make us harsh judges, within habits which make us feel safe, while at our door people are starving and Jesus does not tire of saying to us: "Give them something to eat" (Mk 6:37). (EG 45, 49)

We could go on citing many more passages like these; *Evangelii Gaudium* is full of them. It is an inspired document, marked by a breath which, as we know, reflects not only the Pope's own thinking, but the long process of ecclesial and spiritual discernment of the Latin American church expressed in the historic Aparecida document of 2007.[3]

A moment of grace

We are now in an extraordinary moment of grace in the life of the church. The papacy of Francis represents and crystallizes an

---

3. Fifth General Conference of the Latin American Episcopate, "Concluding Document": celam.org/aparecida/Ingles.pdf.

awareness that he himself expressed: "We cannot passively and calmly wait in our church buildings" (EG 15). We "cannot leave things as they presently are" (EG 25).

His papacy represents the awareness of the need for a reform in the church, and it is interesting to note that while there are voices that persist in denying such need, Pope Francis constantly returns to this as evidence of a crisis, a crisis that is not only institutional and cultural but related to the very nature of the church:

> The Second Vatican Council presented ecclesial conversion as openness to a constant self-renewal born of fidelity to Jesus Christ: "Every renewal of the Church essentially consists in an increase of fidelity to her own calling. . . . Christ summons the Church as she goes her pilgrim way . . . to that continual reformation of which she always has need, in so far as she is a human institution here on earth" (*Unitatis Redintegratio* 6).
>
> There are ecclesial structures which can hamper efforts at evangelization, yet even good structures are only helpful when there is a life constantly driving, sustaining and assessing them. Without new life and an authentic evangelical spirit, without the Church's "fidelity to her own calling," any new structure will soon prove ineffective. (EG 26)

There has been talk of a "new evangelization" for over thirty years now, but the reality has been one of inexorable numerical decline, an ongoing emptying of our churches, a growing irrelevance of Christianity from a cultural point of view, and, worse still, a growing corruption and counter-witness in our institutions. Even monasteries have been heavily marked by these same dynamics. Though there are communities that, thankfully, still prosper today, so many others have unfortunately entered a state of fighting for survival, incapable of renewing themselves, suffering continuous defections, in the grip of an apparently unstoppable decline.

Many have tried to attribute responsibility for this decline to the Second Vatican Council, and we watched this develop, powerless and dismayed, in the first decade of this second millennium, to the point that an Italian historian does not hesitate to refer, somewhat provocatively, to a "Church of the Anti-Council."[4]

That is, until the unexpected gust of evangelical freshness that broke into the church with the election of Pope Francis. Today we are experiencing a moment of grace, an unexpected positive juncture. On one hand, the ecclesial situation had precipitated to such a point that everyone recognized the need for reform, that things could not be allowed to continue as they were (cf. EG 25). On the other hand, the advent of a new, non-European model of evangelization and ecclesial life has begun to break the obsolete and formalistic approaches in which we were caught.

There is an authentically prophetic breath in this new model, a newness that gives hope. It does not seek solutions in a return to the past, but in a renewed relationship with the Gospel—that is, with the risen Lord and with his Spirit. It does not rely on institutional solutions, but on a process of discernment, purification, and reform and a pastoral and missionary conversion, expressed in two programmatic passages of *Evangelii Gaudium*:

> To make this missionary impulse ever more focused, generous and fruitful, I encourage each particular Church [that is, each community] to undertake a resolute process of discernment, purification and reform. (EG 30)

> I hope that all communities will devote the necessary effort to advancing along the path of a pastoral and missionary conversion which cannot leave things as they presently are. "Mere administration" can no longer be enough. Throughout the world, let us be "permanently in a state of mission." (EG 25)

It is therefore important that we allow ourselves to be reached and provoked by this prophetic breath, to let ourselves be drawn

---

4. Giovanni Miccoli, *La Chiesa dell'anticoncilio: I tradizionalisti alla riconquista di Roma* (Rome: Laterza, 2011).

by it into the necessary process of discernment, purification, and reform of our monastic communities, so as not to let this *kairos*, this moment of grace, this favorable juncture pass in vain.

A first step in this requires that we ask ourselves in what ways *Evangelii Gaudium* can actually be applied to monastic life. Monks and nuns, with legitimate exceptions, are generally not directly involved in pastoral care, mission, and evangelization. It might seem therefore that the passages examined so far do not apply directly to monasteries and that it would be difficult to find there a response and solutions to the crisis of our communities today.

The present crisis

To look for an answer to this question, we'll proceed by stages. Let's start by considering this question: Do the reasons for the crisis in our monastic communities run parallel to those related to crisis now experienced in the entire church that Pope Francis diagnoses in *Evangelii Gaudium*? Here are some passages that describe these reasons for crisis:

> The great danger in today's world, pervaded as it is by consumerism, is the desolation and anguish born of a complacent yet covetous heart, the feverish pursuit of frivolous pleasures, and a blunted conscience. Whenever our interior life becomes caught up in its own interests and concerns, there is no longer room for others, no place for the poor. God's voice is no longer heard, the quiet joy of his love is no longer felt, and the desire to do good fades. This is a very real danger for believers too. Many fall prey to it, and end up resentful, angry and listless. That is no way to live a dignified and fulfilled life; it is not God's will for us, nor is it the life in the Spirit which has its source in the heart of the risen Christ. (EG 2)

> The spiritual life comes to be identified with a few religious exercises which can offer a certain comfort but which do not encourage encounter with others, engagement with the

world or a passion for evangelization. As a result, one can observe in many agents of evangelization, even though they pray, a heightened individualism, a crisis of identity and a cooling of fervor. These are three evils which fuel one another. (EG 78)

The other [danger] is the self-absorbed promethean neopelagianism of those who ultimately trust only in their own powers and feel superior to others because they observe certain rules or remain intransigently faithful to a particular Catholic style from the past. A supposed soundness of doctrine or discipline leads instead to a narcissistic and authoritarian elitism, whereby instead of evangelizing, one analyzes and classifies others, and instead of opening the door to grace, one exhausts his or her energies in inspecting and verifying. In neither case is one really concerned about Jesus Christ or others. (EG 94)

This insidious worldliness is evident in a number of attitudes which appear opposed, yet all have the same pretense of "taking over the space of the Church." In some people we see an ostentatious preoccupation for the liturgy, for doctrine and for the Church's prestige, but without any concern that the Gospel have a real impact on God's faithful people and the concrete needs of the present time. In this way, the life of the Church turns into a museum piece or something which is the property of a select few. (EG 95)

Those who have fallen into this worldliness look on from above and afar, they reject the prophecy of their brothers and sisters, they discredit those who raise questions, they constantly point out the mistakes of others and they are obsessed by appearances. . . . [T]hey neither learn from their sins nor are they genuinely open to forgiveness. This is a tremendous corruption disguised as a good. (EG 97)

We don't need to comment on these passages at length. They lucidly describe the situation not only of the church but also of monastic communities. They help us see the need to invest ourselves fully and generously in this process of "discernment, purification, and reform" and in the "pastoral and missionary conversion" to which *Evangelii Gaudium* calls us. We must not lose this *kairos*, this favorable moment. The Holy Spirit has unexpectedly awakened a dynamism in the church today. We must allow ourselves to be touched by this breath of freshness, not just personally but in our communities. Its impact may surprise us. Pope Francis tells us what might happen: "Whenever we make the effort to return to the source and to recover the original freshness of the Gospel, new avenues arise, new paths of creativity open up, with different forms of expression, more eloquent signs and words with new meaning for today's world. Every form of authentic evangelization is always 'new'" (EG 11).

The right motivation

The important thing, however, is to do it the right way, for the right reason, with the right attitude, and in accordance with our charism, our identity. A second step in our analysis consists in asking another question: Why should we undertake this journey? It is important to ask ourselves this in order to avoid the first pitfall of any attempt at renewal in the church—that is, to rely on motivations and dynamisms that are both illusory and harmful for the spiritual life, such as a sense of guilt, an arid legalism, or a self-preservation reflex in our communities or institutions. There has been no lack of attempts at renewal in the church in recent decades, but many of them have failed because they have not been able to draw inspiration from an authentically evangelical dynamism. *Evangelii Gaudium* immediately and resolutely points to this evangelical dynamism, starting from its very title and opening lines: "The joy of the gospel fills the hearts and lives of all who encounter Jesus. Those who accept his offer of salvation are set free from sin, sorrow, inner emptiness and loneliness. With Christ joy is constantly born anew" (EG 1).

A renewal is authentically evangelical only if it is motivated, sustained, and nourished by this joy. When our institutions and communities lose their fervor, their dynamism, and dry up, the heaviest price paid is the sadness, inner emptiness, and sense of sterility; the loneliness that leads to anxiety, depression, or flight; resentment and anger; the fracturing that comes from a climate of slander, jealousy, and competition. Nothing is sadder than visiting a monastic community where one feels unwelcome because there is no mutual acceptance; no one smiles; the liturgy is poor, purely formal, and celebrated out of a sense of habit or duty; and both the people and structures have a shabby appearance.

Is this really what we want? Is that why we gave our lives? How can we resign ourselves to these forms of survival when we know we have been called to life, to bear fruit in abundance, to receive the joy and peace of Christ? Do we not have the desire to regain this life, this fruitfulness, this joy, this peace? Do we not have the desire to rediscover the community dynamism, the kind of vitality we see in so many newer ecclesial realities where, despite some problems, this joy of the Gospel is transmitted and radiated? *Evangelii Gaudium* invites us to return to the Gospel to rediscover this joy and, thanks to it, to find a new breath at the ecclesial level.

What is the Gospel?

But this invitation makes sense only if we understand this Gospel to which Pope Francis points us. We read from its pages every day; we hear about it in homilies regularly; and at least in theory, *lectio divina* is at the center of our spiritual lives—although perhaps we are one of the many people who find ourselves bored rather than inspired by Scripture. If the secret of joy is there, why do we have so much trouble finding it?

The choice of the word *gospel* to designate the literary genre chosen to transmit in written form the apostolic testimony about Jesus refers to Isaiah. The gospel, the "joyful news" that the Lord asks Isaiah to preach to his people, consists in this: "Comfort, give comfort to my people, says your God. / Speak to the heart of Jerusalem" (Isa 40:1-2); "The spirit of the LORD God is upon me, / because the LORD has anointed me; / He has sent me to bring good news to the afflicted, / to bind up the brokenhearted, / To proclaim liberty to the captives, / release to the prisoners, / To announce a year of favor from the LORD" (Isa 61:1-2). This means that the four evangelists' stories, and Scripture in general, become "gospel" only when we allow God to speak through them to our hearts and to console us by wrapping our wounds, freeing us from our prisons, and inaugurating a time of grace, a favorable moment in which the newness of the divine life can break into our lives and the lives of our communities.

This is the gospel spoken of by Pope Francis, and this is why he can associate it inseparably with the joy of salvation. It is also on the basis of this understanding of the Gospel that we appreciate how and in what way evangelization is a reality that concerns monastics just as much as, and maybe even more than, every other Christian.

The Gospel is not just a written text or a set of facts we must believe. It is first and foremost the act through which Christ speaks to our heart, consoles us, encourages us, that is, through which he reaches us with his good news, his joyful announcement, and thus ignites joy in us. This is why Pope Francis emphasizes the *joy* of the Gospel—because only joy is the sign that it is not simply a human message, but it is actually *gospel*, "a joyous announcement" that we have heard. Joy is the sign that we have truly allowed ourselves to be evangelized. "The Church does not evangelize unless she constantly lets herself be evangelized" (EG 174), says Pope Francis, which can be paraphrased in this way: "The church cannot transmit joy if she has not first of all let herself be joyful; the church cannot speak to the hearts of others if she did not first let God speak to her heart; the church cannot console if she has not first allowed herself to be consoled."

This is the primary object of the discernment, purification, and reform to which we are invited, and it is the key to pastoral and missionary conversion. The church gives only what it receives. When it ceases to receive, the church no longer knows how to give; it fails. When it no longer allows itself to be evangelized, it becomes sterile and dry, incapable of evangelizing. When it no longer allows itself to be fed—that is, to be carried upon the shoulders of its one and only Shepherd—it becomes incapable of being pastoral, of feeding the flock. And when it forgets the fundamental truth of its mission, it ceases to be missionary.

Regarding this key truth of mission, there is a misunderstanding to be resolved. There is a fatal forgetfulness that compromises the missionary activity of the church at its foundation, despite the best intentions. The missionary mandate that Jesus gave his disciples just before his ascension is well known: "All power in heaven and on earth has been given to me. Go, therefore, and make disciples of all nations, baptizing them in the name of the Father, and of the Son, and of the holy Spirit, teaching them to observe all that I have commanded you" (Matt 28:18-20). The problem is that we constantly forget the conclusion of this verse: "And behold, I am with you always, until the end of the age" (Matt 28:20). Only because Jesus is with us can we go forth and preach and make disciples. Until they discovered "Jesus with them," the apostles remained closed up, frightened, paralyzed in a room; only after they discovered the resurrection, "Jesus with them," did they receive the freedom, boldness, and joy that made them convincing witnesses to the Gospel!

Monasteries and evangelization

The sense in which monastics are directly involved in evangelization, in this pastoral and missionary conversion of the church, now becomes clear. The key to evangelization and to the pastoral and missionary activity of the church is for Christians, Christian communities, and the entire church to first allow themselves to be evangelized, to be fed, to be guided by the Risen One. The powerful evangelizing, pastoral, and missionary thrust that Pope

Francis is giving to the church consists first in this *letting oneself be evangelized*. Now, the monastic charism has always understood itself exactly in this way with its *nihil operi Dei praeponatur*— "nothing is to be preferred to the Work of God" (RB 43.3). This principle doesn't mean "nothing is more important than the celebration of the liturgy." We speak of *opus Dei* rather than *opus hominis*, because it is not something that *we* do, but that God does! *Nihil operi Dei praeponatur* means "nothing is more important than receiving the work through which *the Lord* constantly speaks to our heart, comforts us, wraps our wounds, frees us from our prisons—in a word, evangelizes us!"

Our contribution as monastics to evangelization is fundamental, because our charism resides precisely in what is at the foundation of evangelization—that is, "letting oneself be evangelized," the "putting nothing before welcoming and celebrating what God does for us" that structures our monastic life.

In this sense, giving priority to the work of God, to letting oneself be evangelized, takes on an irreplaceable ecclesial value because it allows us to experience the deepest aspect of the church's identity. The Second Vatican Council expressed this identity when it taught in *Lumen Gentium*, "the church, in Christ, is a sacrament—a sign and instrument, that is, of communion with God and of the unity of the entire human race."[5]

The church is a sacrament not primarily as an *instrument* of God's salvation through the ordained ministry or the administration of the sacraments; the church is a sacrament first of all because it is a *sign* of the intimate union with God and of the unity of the whole human race, which means that it announces salvation, reconciliation, the covenant, because in it these realities have a certain visibility. The nature of a sign is to make something perceivable, visible. *How* salvation becomes visible, *how* the church acts as a sign, Jesus revealed when he said, "This is how all will

---

5. LG 1. Cf. Luigi Gioia, *La Chiesa: Popolo di Dio in cammino nella storia: La Costituzione dogmatica sulla Chiesa Lumen gentium* (Todi: Tau Editrice, 2015).

know that you are my disciples, if you have love for one another" (John 13:35). That is, they will know it from the quality of your fraternal charity, your community life, your love for one another. In this way, our monasteries become fundamental agents of evangelization. In this lies the heart of our contribution to the pastoral and missionary conversion of the church.

Not just cosmetics

The ideas we have considered so far are certainly important. They speak in one way or another to our hearts, giving us the desire to live something deeper, more beautiful, more authentic in our communities and in our personal and communal relationship with the Lord. But we need to take another step forward, in a direction suggested to us in one of the most compelling sections of Pope Francis's apostolic exhortation: "Progress in building a people in peace, justice and fraternity depends on four principles . . . [which] derive from the pillars of the Church's social doctrine . . . [and] which can guide the development of life in society and the building of a people where differences are harmonized within a shared pursuit" (EG 221).

To help understand how this relates to our topic, in the passage above, let's replace "a people" with "a community." Let's do it also in the following passage: "Becoming a [community] . . . is an ongoing process in which every new generation must take part: a slow and arduous effort calling for a desire for integration and a willingness to achieve this through the growth of a peaceful and multifaceted culture of encounter" (EG 220).

Evangelii Gaudium sets out four principles that can help promote peace in the church and in each of our communities. To speak only of peace might not seem like much to us, but we need to understand what the Pope means by this word. Peace is the result of the integral development of all, the harmonization of all within a common process (cf. EG 219, 221). Ultimately, peace is the context in which one can live freely and find joy and serenity because a balance has been reached between the common good and personal fulfillment.

Now, the third of the four principles Pope Francis presents is this: "Realities are more important than ideas." This warns us of the danger of "dwell[ing] in the realm of words alone, of images and rhetoric" (EG 231), where ideas and knowledge have no impact on reality. They become empty rhetoric—or as the Pope says, "cosmetics," citing Plato's *Gorgias*—instead of real commitment ("real care for our bodies" or, in the original Spanish version, "exercise") (EG 232). He writes, "Not to put the word into practice, not to make it reality, is to build on sand, to remain in the realm of pure ideas and to end up in a lifeless and unfruitful self-centeredness and Gnosticism" (EG 233). The problem, of course, is not the ideas themselves but the fact that we hide behind them and make them alibis, forms of "masking reality" (EG 231) through which "the truth is manipulated" (EG 232).

I will never forget the comment offered to me by a member of another religious order, during a conversation about Benedictine monasticism, "The main defect of Benedictine monasticism," he said, "is that it aims at perfection in form rather than in purpose." He was referring to a tendency in our monasteries that is not uncommon: from the moment we have a well-defined schedule, due attention to liturgy, a neat and clean monastery, well-written constitutions, and so on, we think we have achieved our purpose. Now, all these things are certainly important, but we can never forget that they are only *means*. The purpose and *goal* of common life is fraternal charity and the integral development of people. The aim is to be signs of this love and of the primacy of the person for the church and for the world. So while the form (liturgy, schedule, constitutions, cleanliness,) is important, it can also, Pope Francis is saying, end up hiding reality, becoming an alibi that distracts us from our purpose. Under the well-ordered surface, the facade, people are left to their sadness, their frustration, their loneliness. This facade can hide a form of communal selfishness, a small world closed in upon itself and incapable of real communion with humanity, with suffering, with the lives of our brothers and sisters with whom we share the world.

So how can we avoid being prisoners of beautiful ideas, external forms, and what Francis calls "cosmetics"? How do we introduce real dynamics of change and conversion into our communities? How do we enter the movement of "discernment, purification, and reform" to which we are invited, not by the Pope, let's be clear, but by the Holy Spirit at this moment in the life of the church?

Vicious circle and virtuous circle

For monastic communities, as for every other ecclesial reality, everything revolves around the authenticity of community life. An important step is to clearly identify the mechanisms that activate the vicious circles in which many communities have unfortunately become enmeshed and seem unable to escape. To propose a way out, let's start with one possible solution inspired by the Rule of Benedict and then integrate into this reflection the other three principles offered by Pope Francis in *Evangelii Gaudium*.

The image is inspired by the opening sentence of chapter 72 of the Rule: "Just as there is a *wicked zeal* of bitterness which separates from God and leads to hell, so there is a *good zeal* which separates from evil and leads to God and everlasting life. This, then, is the good zeal which monks must foster with fervent love" (RB 72.1-2, emphasis added). We might paraphrase this as follows: Just as there is a *vicious circle* that separates one from God and leads to sadness, loneliness, and frustration, so there is also a *virtuous circle* that neutralizes negative mechanisms and leads to God and joy, to individual and community self-realization, and to a community becoming a sign of God's salvation for the world; this virtuous circle is what monastics must promote with the most ardent charity and the most lively imagination.

Contemporary leadership studies have long taught us that the mechanisms that determine the success or failure of a community harmonize profoundly with the wisdom of the Rule expressed here. Community reform does not take place by force—for example, by strengthening discipline or surveillance, or by reducing personal freedom; nor is it achieved by sending away difficult people, except, of course, in extreme cases. Rather, it is a question of establishing a dynamism, a new process, of passing precisely from a vicious circle to a virtuous circle and, paradoxically, this kind of change of direction, this *metanoia*, this conversion sometimes depends on small things, like a train that, however large, changes tracks thanks to a small lever that is shifted in the right way at the right time.

From self-defense to trust

Here we encounter the first of the four principles of reform of a community offered by Pope Francis, which he calls "Time is greater than space":

> *Giving priority to space* means madly attempting to keep everything together in the present, trying to possess all the spaces of power and of self-assertion; it is to crystallize processes and presume to hold them back. *Giving priority to time* means being concerned about initiating processes rather than possessing spaces. What we need, then, is to give priority to actions which generate new processes in [community] . . . to the point where they bear fruit. . . . Without anxiety, but with clear convictions and tenacity. [It is about] generating processes of [community]-building, as opposed to obtaining immediate results which yield easy, quick short-term political gains, but do not enhance human fullness. (EG 223–224, emphasis added)

This means that there are actions that paralyze the process of change and actions that activate and nurture it. And if we wanted to identify the fundamental attitude that allows us to move from the vicious circle to the virtuous circle at both the community level and the personal level, if we wanted to label what generates dynamisms instead of paralyzing them, the most correct answer would surely be *trust*.

Secular expertise on leadership is here in full agreement with monastic wisdom and more broadly with the ecclesial vision represented by the social doctrine of the church: no group functions well if mutual trust is lacking. And trust must be earned, built, won, allowing the person and the community to overcome fear, suspicion, the need to protect oneself from others, self-defense.

The portrait of a dysfunctional community can be described as follows:[6]

1) If there is a lack of spaces and incentives for mutual understanding and self-understanding, one cannot trust others and so one seeks to protect oneself as much as possible, *shutting oneself up in a stance of self-defense.*

2) Consequently, when we work on a common project and members of the community are invited to say what they really think, *nobody dares to take a stand*, because there is fear of conflict. Even the superior is afraid of conflict, and the members of the community perceive this and remain closed in on themselves.

3) But if there is no possibility of authentic and honest exchange, because there is no mutual trust and no one takes a stand, then *nobody commits themselves either*, nobody really invests in the common project.

4) Then the communal project falters, everyone does only the bare minimum, and *no one feels responsible.* I don't hold others accountable so that others don't hold me accountable, and we can do all whatever we want undisturbed.

6. Cf. Patrick Lencioni, *The Five Dysfunctions of a Team: A Leadership Fable* (San Francisco: Jossey-Bass, 2002).

5) But if the only glue of a community is the tacit agreement that we all want to be left to do our own thing undisturbed, the price we pay will be solitude, lack of authentic solidarity, frustration, and often anger and the inevitable seeking gratification outside the community and at the expense of the community.

It is clear that we are dealing with a chain, a process, a vicious circle: Because we don't trust each other, we don't dare to take a stand; because we don't dare to take a stand, we don't commit ourselves; because we don't commit ourselves, we don't feel responsible; because we don't feel responsible, no real community is built, people take refuge in individualism, joy disappears, and slander, suspicion, and sadness prevail.

The good news, though, is that because it is a chain, a process, then (as in the example of a train), if you identify the lever that allows you to reverse the mechanism, and if you operate it in the right way and at the right moment, you can then initiate a virtuous circle (a "good zeal") that will progressively affect all the other levels. The lever that accomplishes this is the shift from self-defense to trust.

The role of the superior in this process is fundamental. This is the person who, above all others, must seek to create and promote a climate and culture where trust can be reborn through listening and attentiveness to people, to individuals. *Evangelii Gaudium* offers valuable encouragement in this:

> Today more than ever we need men and women who, on the basis of their experience of accompanying others, are familiar with processes which call for prudence, understanding, patience and docility to the Spirit. . . . We need to practice the art of listening, which is more than simply hearing. Listening, in communication, is an openness of heart which makes possible that closeness without which genuine spiritual encounter cannot occur. Listening helps us to find the right gesture and word which shows that we are more than

simply bystanders. Only through such respectful and compassionate listening can we enter on the paths of true growth and awaken a yearning for the Christian ideal: the desire to respond fully to God's love and to bring to fruition what he has sown in our lives. . . . Reaching a level of maturity where individuals can make truly free and responsible decisions calls for much time and patience. . . .

What the Holy Spirit mobilizes is not an unruly activism, but above all an attentiveness which considers the other "in a certain sense as one with ourselves." This loving attentiveness is the beginning of a true concern for their person which inspires me effectively to seek their good. . . . True love is always contemplative, and permits us to serve the other not out of necessity or vanity, but rather because he or she is beautiful above and beyond mere appearances. . . . Only on the basis of this real and sincere closeness can we properly accompany the poor on their path of liberation. (EG 171, 199)

The good news for superiors is that secular expertise on leadership today recognizes that good leaders do not need to be extroverted, gifted, and charismatic; such people are often impatient, don't know how to listen, and push more than they accompany. Rather, we need introverted leaders, people aware of their limitations but, precisely for this reason, often more effective because they value shared responsibility, leave space for others, and welcome the gifts of all.[7]

Handling dissent

Together with trust, the other decisive lever that opens the way to progress in the church and in our communities is conflict management. We recall the surprise of many when Pope Francis made this request at the beginning of the synod of bishops on the family in 2014:

7. Cf. Susan Cain, *Quiet: The Power of Introverts in a World That Can't Stop Talking* (New York: Crown, 2012).

One general and basic condition is this: speaking honestly. Let no one say: "I cannot say this, they will think this or this of me. . . ." It is necessary to say with *parrhesia* all that one feels. After the last Consistory (February 2014), in which the family was discussed, a Cardinal wrote to me, saying: what a shame that several Cardinals did not have the courage to say certain things out of respect for the Pope, perhaps believing that the Pope might think something else. This is not good, this is not *synodality*, because it is necessary to say all that, in the Lord, one feels the need to say: without polite deference, without hesitation. And, at the same time, one must listen with humility and welcome, with an open heart, what your brothers say. *Synodality* is exercised with these two approaches.[8]

While this attitude has aroused much hope among those who have long sought an effective exercise of synodality within the church, which has been given only lip service until now, it has also caused fear and consternation among those who believe that communion consists in a bland and uniform facade, preserving the impression of agreement, leaving all criticism unexpressed, preventing any sincere, constructive, and honest debate. Many fears were expressed that Francis's approach was rash and that the Pope had lost control of the situation or underestimated the consequences of his invitation.

It is enough, though, to return to the principles for community-building offered in *Evangelii Gaudium* to realize how fully aware Pope Francis is of what he does and of the processes that it triggers. Let us consider, for example, what he says about conflict, dissent, and criticism:

Conflict cannot be ignored or concealed. It has to be faced.
. . . When conflict arises, some people simply look at it and

---

8. Pope Francis, "Greeting to the Synod Fathers during the First General Congregation of the Third Extraordinary General Assembly of the Synod of Bishops," October 6, 2014: http://w2.vatican.va/content/francesco/en/speeches /2014/october/documents/papa-francesco_20141006_padri-sinodali.html.

go their way as if nothing happened; they wash their hands of it and get on with their lives. Others embrace it in such a way that they become its prisoners; they lose their bearings, project onto institutions their own confusion and dissatisfaction and thus make unity impossible. But there is also a third way, and it is the best way to deal with conflict. It is the willingness to face conflict head on, to resolve it and to make it a link in the chain of a new process. "Blessed are the peacemakers!" (Mt 5:9). (EG 226–227)

Nobody likes having to handle conflict, especially a superior. This is so first of all because nobody likes to be challenged, to be held accountable, and also because the expression of dissent opens a door to the unknown, where outcomes are not guaranteed and risks are involved. But risks are inevitable; they are part of life. Life is conflict; movement is conflict— hopefully conflict that is resolved, constructively oriented, but still conflict. Those who try to suppress conflict suffocate life and generate frustrations that then risk producing even more harmful effects. Of course, there are stubborn and deadly dissensions in our communities that are intended not to build, but to destroy. These dissensions are unavoidable and will always express themselves, either openly or through underground whispering. It would be a pity if only harmful dissensions succeeded in imposing themselves because the expression of constructive criticism was not allowed.

The important thing is not to discourage variety, diversity, open and passionate debate. Listening to all the voices can sometimes be uncomfortable, but in the end they always enrich the community and allow everyone to feel heard and co-responsible.

Reconciled diversity

In conclusion, we can return to the question of the contribution to evangelization and the pastoral and missionary conversion of the church to which *Evangelii Gaudium* calls monastics.

We saw that the heart of our monastic vocation, the "nothing is to be preferred to the Work of God" of the Rule of Benedict, means allowing the covenant, reconciliation, communion to be expressed and become visible in a life that actually becomes a sign of this grace, whose nature is essentially community. If this is the grace we receive, if we actually welcome it with an open and sincere heart, then it will become visible in the quality and fruitfulness of our community life. It will shape our community into a sign of salvation, a visible place of salvation in the church and, thanks to this, an agent of evangelization.

So much could be said to describe the nature of a community that truly allows itself to be evangelized, that opens itself to the joy of the Gospel. Here, in conclusion, we will mention two points from *Evangelii Gaudium*: first, on reconciled diversity and second, an image of Francis's that has become well known, the polyhedron.

"The message of peace," Pope Francis writes, "is not about a negotiated settlement but rather the conviction that the unity brought by the Spirit can harmonize every diversity. It overcomes every conflict by creating a new and promising synthesis. Diversity is a beautiful thing when it can constantly enter into a process of reconciliation and seal a sort of cultural covenant resulting in a 'reconciled diversity'" (EG 230).

Nothing is more encouraging than when, upon visiting a community, one immediately perceives the different personalities, experiences the diversity, and sees that each person's gifts and qualities are fully welcomed and freely expressed, even if the dynamics may appear a little chaotic or, to recall Pope Francis's expression again, even though "our lives become wonderfully complicated" (EG 270).

To visualize this model of "reconciled diversity," *Evangelii Gaudium* offers—in the fourth and final of the Pope's four key principles, "The whole is greater than the part"—the eloquent image of the polyhedron: "People who wholeheartedly enter into the life of a community [do not] need to lose their individualism or hide their identity; instead, they receive new impulses to personal growth. The global need not stifle, nor the particular prove barren. . . . Here our model is not the sphere, which is no greater than its parts, where every point is equidistant from the center, and there are no differences between them. Instead, it is the polyhedron, which reflects the convergence of all its parts, each of which preserves its distinctiveness" (EG 235–236).

When you rotate a polyhedron, you see different shapes and colors, maybe even contrasting ones, yet the polyhedron remains unique and these shapes harmonize and adapt to each other. Of course, the process of integrating such different forms can be long and laborious, and it will often be necessary to smooth a corner that is a bit sharp. But it will have been worth it, because the unity gained in this way does not erase people's ideas and personalities, but enhances their diversity and is the only form of unity that the modern mentality is willing to accept, the only one in which it is willing to invest.

The key to everything, however, is to find and operate the lever that triggers the virtuous circle, to start the right process—that is, to promote a climate of community in which, gradually, one after another, members can move from self-defense to trust.

CHAPTER XII

Monastic Wisdom

*The incarnation is fraught with ambiguity. It is not
a "triumphant epiphany," but the shipwreck of one
particular human life, a life in which God willingly
endures the emptiness of history. Faith, then, is never
a means of escaping the torment of a bleak world;
rather faith endures that torment, finding within the
world an ambiguous disclosure of meaning.*

Benjamin Myers (describing the thought
of Rowan Williams)[1]

The monastic contribution to theology has often been called
"sapiential."[2] The word suggests a search not only to understand
the realities of faith but above all for the experience of those realities. Usually, the meaning of this expression is explained with the
help of its etymology: coming from the Latin word *sapere* ("to
taste"), a sapiential way of reading Scripture consists not only
in the effort to comprehend it but above all in the desire to be

---

1. Benjamin Myers, *Christ the Stranger: The Theology of Rowan Williams* (London: T&T Clark, 2012), 24.

2. Cf., for example, Elmar Salmann, ed., *La teologia mistico-sapienziale di
Anselm Stolz*, Studia Anselmiana 100 (Rome: Centro Studi S. Anselmo, 1988);
Benedetto Calati, *Sapienza monastica: Saggi di storia, spiritualità e problemi mo-
nastici*, Studia Anselmiana 107 (Rome: Centro studi S. Anselmo, 1994).

nourished by it, to taste it. In this way, however, we try to explain one metaphor ("sapiential") through recourse to others ("experience," "taste") without providing any greater conceptual clarity. So *sapiential* is a description that, however suggestive, is difficult to handle. A more rewarding attempt to clarify it consists in turning to the Old Testament literature that is also known as sapiential or, better, to the sapiential vein that runs through the whole of Scripture. We'll then take the further step of pointing out the echoes of this sapiential vein in two of the major documents of the Second Vatican Council, *Lumen Gentium* and *Gaudium et Spes*. On this basis, it will be possible to better appreciate what is meant by talking of the monastic contribution to a sapiential way of doing theology.

The liberating power of faith

In his famous prayer imploring the gift of wisdom, Solomon asked for "a listening heart . . . to distinguish between good and evil" (1 Kgs 3:9). The twentieth-century Old Testament scholar Gerhard von Rad wrote of this:

> What [Solomon], the paradigm of the wise man, wished for himself was not the authoritative reason which reigns supreme over a dead natural matter, the reason of modern consciousness, but an "understanding" reason, a feeling for the truth which emanates from the world and addresses man. He was totally receptive to that truth, but this was not passivity, but an intense activity, the object of which was response, prudent articulation. The discovery of truth on the basis of the modern concept of reason, on the other hand, is, rather, an experience of power. It produces an ability to control. . . . [It] is technically determined. . . . [It is] in opposition to the receptivity of wisdom and equally hostile to any attainment of trust.[3]

3. Gerhard von Rad, *Wisdom in Israel* (Nashville: Abingdon Press, 1972), 296–297.

Negatively, therefore, "sapiential" means the rejection of an authoritarian reason, one that controls, is technically determined, and whose activity is an exercise of power. Positively, it describes a reason that listens to itself and to the world, is characterized by a certain humility, and is therefore skeptical of "attempting great, sweeping explanations."[4]

It is significant that access to such reason is sought not only through study, research, and intellectual effort, but above all through prayer. Such a capacity for listening and such humility require a freedom that Solomon knew he could draw on only through his faith in the Lord, in the one and inscrutable God who cannot be known but with whom it is possible to enter into a covenant relationship because he has made himself "God with us," a God above all gods, all the phenomena of nature, and all that exists.

It is difficult for us to understand what liberating power the ancients found in faith in the Lord as creator of heaven and earth and all that exists. As long as they were caught in a mythical conception of the origin of the cosmos (for example, the various cosmologies that conceived the world as the fruit of the marriage of gods or as the result of the dismemberment of gods), they were imprisoned in an animistic vision of reality and tended to sacralize the world. By personifying natural phenomena and not knowing the intention of the many divinities behind them, the ancients were afraid of everything, and sacrifice developed precisely as a form of barter aimed at propitiating with blood these faceless agents, to try to tame their power. We perhaps do not realize well enough how myth is a form of narrative ideology—it resorts to an invented *narrative* that offers an *explanation* of, for example, the origin of the world or a people or a ritual or modes of behavior, whose authority depends on the *sacredness* attributed to it, generally validated by its *antiquity*. It is therefore an explanation that excuses from asking real questions and from the duty to seek

4. Von Rad, 310.

solutions, and for this very reason it becomes a formidable instrument of power (which is why it is a form of ideology).

Faith in the Lord of Israel cuts the Gordian knot of mythology at the root, because it establishes an absolute distinction between creator and creature and therefore opens the way to a desacralized view of the world and of the course of events. In this sense we can consider "the wisdom practiced in Israel [to be] a response made by a Yahwism confronted with specific experiences of the world."[5] The believer, thanks to this faith, acquires the freedom to question the world and the course of history without fear, seeking its meaning in the context of the relationship with the Lord. In this way, "to radical secularization of the world there corresponded the idea of an equally radical domination of the world by Yahweh, that is the idea of the world as a creation of Yahweh."[6]

The "sapiential" attitude toward reason that results from this faith and this freedom therefore lies in the extraordinary possibility of taking an interest in the world *as world*, serenely accepting its secularity: "Dissociating itself sharply from a sacral understanding of the world, this way of thinking placed man and his created environment in a measure of secularity. . . . With wonderful open-mindedness, the old teachers' way of thinking circles round a man who has been, to a certain extent, newly discovered, a man with all his psychological realities and imponderables, his possibilities and his limitations."[7]

We are speaking here, of course, within the framework of a theological definition of secularity. It is not a space that excludes God, but, on the contrary, a place where one can live peacefully only thanks to faith in God because it has been freed from sacrality, from belief in a divinity that is everywhere and that would manifest itself in the *tremendum* (the awe and terror inspired by the divinity, the demonic dread). Faith frees the believer from

5. Von Rad, 307.
6. Von Rad, 298.
7. Von Rad, 316–317.

fear, from sacral terror. In the liberated world, thanks to faith, we are not worried when God's presence and action are not obvious or explicit. Wisdom is not produced by signs of divine intervention; it does not seek spectacular confirmation in the phenomena of nature or in extraordinary revelations. It seeks to understand the presence and action of God in the cosmos and in history by understanding humanity:

> In Prov. 10–29 . . . the objects, particularly the experiences of community life, are understood in a predominantly "secular" way, or, to be more precise, the environment is addressed, in characteristically dialectic terms, as a secular entity governed by Yahweh. . . . [K]nowledge about Yahweh enabled one to understand the world as world. . . . The thinking of the wise men was never, from the very beginning, stimulated by signs of divine activity in history. Rather, they felt themselves stimulated above all by the much older question of humanity . . . [and] of human existence. . . . Israel only knew a related man, related to other men, to his environment and, not least, to God.[8]

We can better understand the nature of this sapiential attitude by comparing it with a *prophetic* one. The prophet experiences the intervention of God in a dramatic way. He is torn from his ordinary life. Speaking in the name of God (the Greek *pro-phanai* means "to speak for, in the name of," hence the name "prophet") is often a burden, a weight, sometimes even carried out unwillingly. Through the prophet, it is God who seeks humanity. The sage (person of wisdom), on the other hand, can be defined as one who, precisely because he has been freed by the Lord, becomes capable of seeking himself, of seeking the other, and almost indirectly of seeking even God: "In wisdom man was in search of himself and took things into his own hands without being able to appeal to a

8. Von Rad, 299, 300, 314, 315.

specific, divine commission. . . . In a word, he strove to discover his humanity in the sphere which had been allotted him by God."[9]

Wisdom presupposes prophecy, but it bears witness to a more mature phase in the relationship with God that integrates greater responsibility, personal decision, and appeal to reason:

> In the form of wisdom instruction, a certain liberality—perhaps in contrast to the "apodeictic" [that is, "incontestable"] divine law—has long been noted. It is directed towards the understanding of the person being instructed; it cannot and will not take away from him the power of decision. Even when man was being urgently addressed, an area was always left which the teacher never entered but which he left free for the pupil to use as he wished. . . . It was then the pupil's task, one might say, correctly to recognize the time in which the sentence is true or in which it becomes false.[10]

One of the most interesting features of wisdom for our investigation is precisely this ability to wait, to allow time to pass, to respect the maturation necessary for decisions to be reached in a responsible and personal manner. In a word, the sapiential attitude is characteristic of a reason that does not seek a conclusion too quickly, because it has learned to take processes and history seriously. It accepts that the emergence of truth requires a long-term, daily contact with life even in its apparently most insignificant characters. It recognizes that meaning appears only through a history that is actually lived, not only "sacred" history, the one in which the intervention of God is clear, but the history of humanity as such.

In summary, we can say that the "sapiential" attitude has the following characteristics:

9. Von Rad, 309.
10. Von Rad, 309, 311.

(1) it rests on the full assumption of a humanity authentically in touch with itself, with history, and with the world;

(2) it is capable of taking an interest in the world as world, without fearing its secularity;

(3) it is capable of resisting the temptation to look for syntheses prematurely, because it has learned to take processes and history seriously.

An authentically sapiential theology and spirituality therefore fully integrate humanity through an active knowledge of the self and take history and the world seriously. In this way we avoid, on one hand, the pitfall of Manichaeism—that is, an externalization and objectification of evil with the parallel temptation of angelism; and on the other hand, the pitfall of Donatism—that is, the anticipation of the eschaton and the claim to be ensconced in a space of truth and justice, standing in a position of judgment with respect to the rest of the world.

A church proclaiming the freedom of God

Our brief consideration of wisdom in Scripture has shown us that cultivating a genuine interest in humanity, taking history seriously, and accepting the secularity of the world, far from being symptoms of the exclusion of God from one's own horizon, are the result of a mature faith in the Lord and a sound understanding of how God relates to creation. In other words, wisdom rests on a high conception of the singularity of divine action and on a clear distinction between, and more intelligent articulation of, this divine action and human action.

With this perspective, we can understand much better two key documents of the Second Vatican Council, the dogmatic constitution on the church, *Lumen Gentium*, and the pastoral constitution on the church in the modern world, *Gaudium et Spes*. In theology, referring to the church is just another way of talking about how the

Father, the Son, and the Holy Spirit act in history. All the crises of the church in its two-thousand-year journey can be traced to a weakening of the primacy of divine action and of the right way to relate to it by trying to appropriate it, exploit it, or confuse it with human action.

For this reason, in the light of the sapiential approach that we are exploring, one of the most instructive interpretations of these conciliar documents is precisely this: *Lumen Gentium* and *Gaudium et Spes*, by reestablishing the primacy of divine action and asserting its freedom, allow us to reach a sounder understanding of the true nature of humanity, the world, and history.

Let us begin, then, by looking at how this emphasis on the primacy of divine action is developed in *Lumen Gentium*.[11] The constitution speaks of the church as a mystery: "The mystery of the holy church is already brought to light in the manner of its foundation" (LG 5); "The church, that is, the kingdom of Christ already present in mystery grows visibly in the world through the power of God" (LG 3). It then affirms that the union of the faithful with Christ in the church, although real, remains *hidden*: "In this body the life of Christ is communicated to those who believe and who, through the sacraments, are united in a hidden and real way to Christ in his passion and glorification" (LG 7). Taking up the vocabulary of Paul, *Lumen Gentium* says again that the life of the church is hidden: "The life of the church is hidden with Christ in God until it appears in glory with its Spouse" (LG 6). In a similar way, at different points *Lumen Gentium* treats the church as an incomplete reality, as something in process, under construction: "[The church was] made manifest in the outpouring of the Spirit, it will be brought to glorious completion at the end of time" (LG 2); "The church . . . will receive its perfection only in the glory of heaven" (LG 48, citing Eph 1:10 and Col 1:20).

---

11. For a more detailed analysis, see Gioia, *La Chiesa*.

To understand better what is behind this guardedness, we can note how it disappears completely when *Lumen Gentium* speaks of Christ: "This kingdom shines out before humanity in the words, the works and the presence of Christ" (LG 5, emphasis mine). While the action of God *in the church* is mysterious, hidden, and incomplete, *in Christ* it is fully manifest. This explains the very title of the constitution: *Lumen Gentium*, "light of the nations." The document's topic is the church, but its title doesn't refer to the church. It is Christ, not the church, who is the light. In fact, the first two words of the constitution, which give it this title, are found in the following passage: "Christ is the light of the nations [*lumen gentium cum sit Christus*] and consequently this holy synod, gathered together in the holy Spirit, ardently desires to bring to all humanity that light of Christ which is resplendent on the face of the church, by proclaiming his Gospel to every creature" (LG 1, emphasis mine).

The words of this first paragraph were chosen with extreme care: Christ is the light of all people; the church reflects this light. That is, the church lives to the extent that it receives this light, remains connected to Christ. The same idea is reiterated later: "All are called to this union with Christ, who is the light of the world, from whom we come, through whom we live, and towards whom we direct our lives" (LG 3). To repeat Barth's effective image, the church is like a neon sign, visible only when electricity passes through it and illuminates it. If there is no electricity, the neon, although it exists, cannot be seen and is indistinguishable from the darkness of the night that surrounds it.

This allows us to understand better the programmatic phrase of the entire document, where the relationship between church and sacrament is established: "The Church is in Christ like [*velut*] a sacrament or as a sign and instrument both of a very closely knit union with God and of the unity of the whole human race" (LG 1).[12]

12. See https://www.vatican.va/archive/hist_councils/ii_vatican_council /documents/vat-ii_const_19641121_lumen-gentium_en.html.

It would be easy to miss the Latin adverb *velut* in this sentence, translated into English here as "like" (and in some translations as "a kind of"). But it has immense theological weight; one could argue that it is the most important word of all the council's teaching. To affirm that the church is a sacrament means that, as the document itself explains, it is a sign and instrument of union with God and of communion among people. The church is a sign because those who see the church see this communion with God and among people; to say that it is an instrument means that this communion with God and among people is accessed through the church. Why then include the *velut* in this definition? Why weaken this claim? Why say that the church is a sign and instrument only "in some way," only "in a certain sense"? The answer is already suggested by calling Christ "the Light of nations," implying that the church does not shine with its own light but only with reflected light. Only Christ is fully a sign; only in him are the kingdom of God and the action of God clearly manifested. Through the church, on the other hand, the kingdom and action of God truly manifest themselves, but in mystery, in a hidden and incomplete way.

To insist on the significance of this *velut* not only doesn't undermine the saving importance of the church; it is actually the only way to grasp the church's true purpose, its true greatness. Only Christ is true light, only he is true sacrament; the church is so to the extent that it remains dependent on Christ and the Holy Spirit. And this dependence must never be taken for granted. It must never be reduced to sacramental efficacy or apostolic succession alone, but hangs on a real and ongoing conversion made possible by a continuous and effective listening to the word of God in faith and in prayer that is manifested in authentic charity.

This context helps us understand the well-known and controversial Latin phrase *subsistit in* that appears in the same document: "This church [as the reality of grace], constituted and organized as a society in the present world, subsists in [*subsistit in*] the Catholic Church [as institution], which is governed by the successor of Peter and by the bishops in communion with him" (LG 8). The

purpose of this passage was to avoid a pure and simple identification between the reality of grace and the visible Catholic
Church. *Subsistit in* means that between the two (reality of grace
and institution) there is certainly a real unity, but it also suggests a
dialectic that characterizes this relationship, exactly like the *velut*
mentioned above.

That this is the authentic meaning of the term is confirmed
by other internal evidence. In fact, the same paragraph of *Lumen
Gentium* continues: "Nevertheless, many elements of sanctification
and of truth are found outside its visible confines. Since these are
gifts belonging to the church of Christ, they are forces impelling
towards catholic unity" (LG 8). If there are elements of sanctification and truth outside the visible limits of the Catholic Church as
an institution, then the church as a reality of grace is not confined
to the institution, but exceeds its limits, even if everything in the
end must flow into the latter. Moreover, it is significant that the
text doesn't say that these elements of sanctification and grace
belong specifically to "the Catholic Church," but to "the Church
of Christ"; and that they don't lead "toward the Catholic Church,"
but "toward catholic unity."

These seemingly slight semantic nuances point to crucial theological truths. An important consequence of these observations is
not only that elements of sanctification and truth are also present
outside the visible limits of the Catholic Church, but also that
these same elements of sanctification and truth are often not fully
present in the Catholic Church itself, as the decree on ecumenism,
Unitatis Redintegratio, states: "For although the Catholic church
has been endowed with all divinely revealed truth and with all
means of grace, yet its members fail to live by them with all the
fervor that they should. As a result, the radiance of the church's
face shines less brightly in the eyes of our separated sisters and
brothers and of the world at large, and the growth of God's kingdom is retarded" (UR 4).

While in its mystery the church is holy, in its members—that
is, in what we experience of it on a daily basis—it is so imperfect

that not only is it not identical with the kingdom of God, but it can even delay and or obstruct the coming of that kingdom.

A church not afraid of history

We can now begin to see the newness of the approach to the church offered by *Lumen Gentium*. To understand the church, we cannot remain on the abstract plane; we must recognize its historicity, which implies a progressive unfolding of its identity. Now, the biblical category that best expresses this approach to the identity of the church is that of *the people of God*.[13] We can't explore the theological meaning of this image of the church in great depth here, but we should at least pause to consider what it implies in two contexts that constitute the theological foundation of *Gaudium et Spes* and that correspond to what we have said about the sapiential approach to reality, namely solidarity with all humanity based on a real insertion into history, on taking that history seriously.

One of the results of understanding the church as the people of God—fruitful not only on a theological level, but also on a spiritual and pastoral level—is the seriousness with which we take the historicity of salvation, that is, its progressive character, with all the pedagogy that this process involves. The Lord forms his people progressively, patiently, slowly: "He therefore chose the people of Israel to be his own people and established a covenant with them. He instructed them gradually, making both himself and his intentions known in the course of their history, and made them holy for himself" (LG 9). Likewise the church, "in order to extend to all regions of the earth, . . . enters into human history,

---

13. LG 13: "All women and men are called to belong to the new people of God. This people therefore, whilst remaining one and unique, is to be spread throughout the whole world and to all ages in order that the design of God's will may be fulfilled: he made human nature one in the beginning and has decreed that all his children who were scattered should be finally gathered together as one."

though it transcends at once all times and all boundaries between peoples" (LG 9); the church is not ashamed that it "carries the mark of this world which will pass," or that "it takes its place among the creatures which groan and until now suffer the pains of childbirth and await the revelation of the children of God" (LG 48). Accepting an authentic solidarity with all humanity and taking history seriously give great freedom to the church and allow it to carry out a role, with respect to those to whom it is sent, not of conquest, but of welcoming, listening, gathering.[14]

Given all of this, it is interesting to note the strange eclipse of the concept of the people of God in theology and, even more, in the official teaching of the church over the past thirty years. It was criticized for being less precise than the notion of the church as the body of Christ, and some tried to replace it with the concept of communion. One can be troubled only by the way the post-conciliar magisterium has distanced itself from the clear intention of the council to emphasize the notion of the church as the people of God. Why has this image aroused such concern? The answer is clear when we consider its key aspects: first, it is founded on the baptismal priesthood, placing the accent on the fundamental equality of all Christians; and second, it takes the church's historicity seriously. In both of these ways, it represents a theological antidote to the clericalism that unfortunately still remains deeply rooted in Catholic culture and teaching. One of the clearest signs of a reversal of this trend has been Pope Francis's unapologetic and straightforward recovery of the concept of the people of God right from the beginning of his pontificate:

14. LG 13: "The church or people of God . . . fosters and takes to itself, in so far as they are good, people's abilities, resources and customs. In so taking them to itself it purifies, strengthens and elevates them. The church, indeed, is mindful that it must gather in along with that King to whom the nations were given for an inheritance (see Ps 2:8) and to whose city they bring gifts and offerings."

The image of the Church that I like is that of the holy, faithful people of God. This is the definition I often use, which is the image of *Lumen gentium*, no. 12. Belonging to a people has a strong theological value. In the history of salvation, God has saved a people. There is no full identity without belonging to a people. No one is saved alone, as an isolated individual, but God attracts us looking at the complex web of relationships that take place in the human community. God enters into this popular dynamic.

The people themselves are the subject. And the Church is the people of God on the journey through history, with joys and sorrows. *Sentire cum Ecclesia* [to think and to feel with the Church], therefore, is my way of being a part of this people. And all the faithful, considered as a whole, are infallible in matters of belief, and the people display this *infallibilitas in credendo*, this infallibility in believing, through a supernatural sense of the faith of all the people walking together.[15]

Elsewhere, Francis said, "The Church is or should go back to being a community of God's people, and priests, pastors and bishops who have the care of souls, are at the service of the people of God."[16]

By rehabilitating the concept of the people of God, the council and, after a gap of fifty years, Pope Francis put the action of God at the center, showing that they do not fear the humanity of the church and thus open the possibility to rethinking the church's and Christians' way of being and acting along three fundamental axes similar to the sapiential vein of Scripture explored above, namely: (1) solidarity with all humanity; (2) the freedom to take

15. Pope Francis with Antonio Spadaro, *My Door Is Always Open: A Conversation on Faith, Hope, and the Church in a Time of Change*, trans. Shaun Whiteside (London: Bloomsbury, 2013), 49–50.

16. Eugenio Scalfari, "The Pope: How the Church Will Change," *L'Espresso*, October 1, 2013: https://www.repubblica.it/cultura/2013/10/01/news/pope_s _conversation_with_scalfari_english-67643118/.

history seriously; (3) the freedom to weave relationships based on listening, dialogue, and welcoming.

The best way to step into *Gaudium et Spes* will therefore be to explore it along these three tracks; this will help us discover its pastoral implications.

A church not afraid of humanity

The basic pastoral consequence of all of this is that Christians are called to, as *Gaudium et Spes* puts it, "work closely with their contemporaries" and "try to understand their ways of thinking and feeling, as these find expression in current culture."[17] This effort should be devoid of any condescendence, because such a "union" must be based on authentic solidarity. Christ certainly came to make us children of God, but he did so by assuming our humanity, becoming fully one of us. The disciple is not greater than the teacher, so the only way we, too, can go to the Father is by following Christ in this same humanization: "To follow Christ the perfect human is to become more human oneself," says *Gaudium et Spes* (41) splendidly.

This is the assumption of the magnificent opening sentence of the constitution. In the decades following the council, *Gaudium et Spes* has often been berated for its alleged naive optimism, and its incipit, "Joys and Hopes," is cited as evidence. But you have to get only as far as the third and fourth words of the same sentence to immediately find reference to "griefs and anxieties" and so realize that the council fathers did not for a moment forget the church's healthy realism and prioritization of those who suffer. *Gaudium et Spes* does not call for an escape from the world or from history, but to measure the authenticity of the Christian identity on the basis of compassion toward all:

17. Second Vatican Council, Pastoral Constitution on the Church in the Modern World *Gaudium et Spes* (hereafter, GS) 62.

The joys and hopes, the grief and anguish of the people of our time, especially of those who are poor or afflicted, are the joys and hopes, the grief and anguish of the followers of Christ as well. Nothing that is genuinely human fails to find an echo in their hearts. For theirs is a community of people united in Christ and guided by the holy Spirit in their pilgrimage towards the Father's kingdom, bearers of a message of salvation for all of humanity. That is why they cherish a feeling of deep solidarity with the human race and its history. (GS 1)

Too often, Christian and monastic spirituality has interpreted the Pauline warning that "the world in its present form is passing away" (1 Cor 7:31) as an excuse to escape from the world and from history. But for *Gaudium et Spes*, "There is no question, then, of the Christian message inhibiting them from building up the world or making them disinterested in the good of others: on the contrary it makes it a matter of stricter obligation" (GS 34). In fact, the document continues, "Far from diminishing our concern to develop this earth, the expectation of a new earth should spur us on, for it is here that the body of a new human family grows" (GS 39).

In light of the biblical sapiential perspective that we are exploring, we might formulate the purpose of the council's *aggiornamento* like this: an authentic spirituality is built only through a full integration of one's own humanity, a humanity that we should not diminish, deny, ignore, or manipulate.

This solidarity does not result from condescension, but from the awareness that even as Christians, as believers in a process of conversion, we are exposed like all our contemporaries to everything that characterizes the human condition, including the nonevidence of God in the world and the constant temptation of an atheism not so much theoretical as practical; the perennial temptation of taking refuge in the sacred (in the form of aestheticism or mysticism) that offers tangible fulfillment and a sense of power; a relationship to time that makes uncertainty about the future a burden, with existential anxiety that no one can fully avoid; and finally, an inevitable complicity with the violence of history, by virtue of which we all contribute to maintaining the structures of sin that generate the evils that afflict the world.[18]

Fullness of meaning only at the end

Aggiornamento, the watchword of the entire conciliar project, has allowed the church to understand itself no longer simply as the guardian of a tradition that comes from the past, but as the sign of the action and the presence of the risen Christ through his Spirit in today's world. According to *Gaudium et Spes*, this vocation leads the church to constantly go out beyond itself to reach all people; "it addresses not only the daughters and sons of the church and all who call upon the name of Christ, but the whole of humanity as well, and it wishes to set down how it understands the presence and function of the church in the world of today. . . . It is the world as the theatre of human history, bearing the marks of its travail, its triumphs and failures" (GS 2).

The church is aware of how "in each nation and social group there is a growing number of men and women who are conscious that they themselves are the architects and molders of their community's culture," and for this reason it wants to contribute to the construction of "a better world in truth and justice"—that is, contributing to "a new humanism, where people are defined before all else by their responsibility to their sisters and brothers and at the court of history" (GS 55).

According to *Gaudium et Spes*, adopting the sapiential attitude of taking history seriously means accepting that the full meaning of history will become clear only at the end of time, only after history has run its course. This means, however, that while history is in progress, before its final meaning is clear, there is room for a variety of provisional and often conflicting interpretations of reality, not because there is no objective and unique meaning to

18. Cf. Jean-Yves Lacoste, *Expérience et absolu* (Paris: Presses Universitaires de France, 1994).

events, but because, due to our historicity, we will have access to this deepest meaning of events only at its end.

But this also implies that the interpretation of historical events is subject to the verification of historical criticism for Christianity exactly as it is for every other human reality. From this point of view, there is no difference, for example, between the claim of Christianity and that of Islam to be the revelation of the true God. Confirmation regarding the truth of Christianity can't be sought in special and direct evidence; it must be awaited until the end of time when the full meaning of events will be made manifest.[19] This does not mean that, as Christians, we do not believe in Christ's claim to be the way, the truth, and the life (cf. John 14:6), but that we also acknowledge that there is a secular space in which this truth is not evident to everyone just as not all of Jesus' contemporaries believed that he was the Son of God and that even the disciples had to struggle a long time before even beginning to grasp the real nature of Jesus' identity.

Refusing polarization

Constantly renewed by faith in a creating and redeeming God who wills the salvation of all people, and thereby freed from magical or sacral thinking, the church, *Gaudium et Spes* teaches, can recognize and respect without fear another sapiential element mentioned above, that is, the legitimate autonomy of earthly realities: "As regards religion, . . . people are taking a hard look at all magical world-views and prevailing superstitions and are demanding a more personal and active commitment of faith, so that not a few have achieved a lively sense of the divine" (GS 7). This more vivid sense of the God of Jesus Christ allows every Christian to fully enjoy freedom from idolatry, from a mythological relationship

19. Cf. Wolfhart Pannenberg, "Tesi dogmatiche sulla dottrina della rivelazione," in Wolfhart Pannenberg, Rolf Rendtorff, Trutz Rendtorff, and Ulrich Wilckens, *Rivelazione come storia* (Bologna: Dehoniane, 1969), 161–195.

with the world, and from a fatalistic relationship with history thanks to his or her faith in the Creator. "If by the autonomy of earthly affairs is meant the gradual discovery, utilization and ordering of the laws and values of matter and society, then the demand for autonomy is perfectly in order: it is at once the claim of humankind today and the desire of the creator" (GS 36). The church must never be afraid of knowledge, because nothing that any genuine research discovers about reality can ever "conflict with the faith, because the things of the world and the things of faith derive from the same God" (GS 36). The council offers an explicit recognition of "how much [the church] has profited from the history and development of humankind. It profits from the experience of past ages, from the progress of the sciences, and from the riches hidden in various cultures, through which greater light is thrown on human nature and new avenues to truth are opened up" (GS 44).

The church thus rediscovers the freedom to develop a relationship with humanity—of which it is a part and to which it is sent—that is neither naive nor wholly oppositional. Here we find more specifically another sapiential attitude, which consists in committing ourselves to discovering our "humanity in the sphere which had been allotted [to us] by God."[20]

The possibility of listening without prejudice, with sincere interest in the other, especially when it is different or even opposed to us, the refusal to yield to polarized versions of reality—these do not develop spontaneously, but require overcoming fear and a liberation that only faith in God allows. The whole spiritual tradition insists that authentic discernment results from this freedom of the children of God. This freedom allows the church to recognize "the good to be found in the social dynamism of today, especially in progress towards unity, healthy socialization, and civil and economic cooperation" (GS 42). In this freedom the church

20. Von Rad, *Wisdom in Israel*, 309.

is aware of the need to "be aware of and understand the aspirations, the yearnings, and the often dramatic features of the world in which we live" (GS 4). The church examines the signs of the times and tries to interpret them in the light of the Gospel (cf. GS 4). "Impelled by that faith, they try to discern the true signs of God's presence and purpose in the events, the needs and the desires which it shares with the rest of humanity today. For faith casts a new light on everything and makes known the full ideal which God has set for humanity, thus guiding the mind towards solutions that are fully human" (GS 11). "With the help of the holy Spirit, it is the task of the whole people of God, particularly of its pastors and theologians, to listen to and distinguish the many voices of our times and to interpret them in the light of God's word, in order that the revealed truth may be more deeply penetrated, better understood, and more suitably presented" (GS 44).

The authenticity of this listening and discernment is manifested especially in the dialogue with those who appear to be opponents or even enemies of the church. The church "sincerely proclaims that all men and women, those who believe as well as those who do not, should help to establish right order in this world where all live together. This certainly cannot be done without a dialogue that is sincere and prudent" (GS 21). Just as Christ never imposed himself by force, but always relied on persuasion, so Christian behavior toward "those who think or act differently than we do in social, political and even religious matters" must be marked by "courtesy and love," because "the more deeply we come to understand their ways of thinking . . . the more easily will we be able to enter into dialogue with them" (GS 28).

One of the most eloquent signs of authentic conversion to the God of Jesus Christ, the new Adam, is a disciple's deeper embrace of humanity and a renewed commitment not only to evangelization but also to collaboration "with everyone for the establishment of a more human world" (GS 57) to help make "the human family and its history still more human" (GS 40). The entire text of *Gaudium et Spes* is imbued with this spirit. The Christian is an assiduous builder of peace, because the Beatitudes promise to peacemakers the happiness of being called children of God (Matt 5:9). But peace in a secular space is built only by actively protecting the good of all people, with "a firm determination to respect the dignity of other individuals and peoples along with the deliberate practice of friendliness" (GS 78). Christians who see themselves as being at war against culture, who marginalize themselves, who are unwilling to contribute as one voice among many others in today's secular and pluralistic culture betray an essential dimension of Christian identity. We do not evangelize by becoming judges of nonbelievers, but by contributing in some form, small or large, to the good of humanity as a whole.

Monasticism and sapiential theology

We have thus far explored what sapiential theology is in the light of both the Old Testament and the conciliar *aggiornamento*. We now need to clarify the monastic contribution to this vision of reality and to this way of relating to God's action. We'll do so along the three axes that we've used to summarize the sapiential approach to theology, namely (1) solidarity, (2) the full recognition of historicity, and (3) magnanimous dialogue. We will proceed in two stages, first conducting a very brief exercise of listening to the signs of the times, in particular with regard to the cultural phenomenon that is usually described as "postmodernism," and then trying to show how the monastic vocation responds to this context and how this response constitutes for the whole church the paradigm of a position toward the world that is not antagonistic, but permeated by the sapiential attitude we're advocating.

Postmodernism

In this exercise of listening to the signs of the times, we will limit ourselves to referring to one undeniable aspect of contemporary culture that seems to express the essence of what we call postmodernity—that is, the fundamental mistrust in the claim of any theory, narrative, or creed to express objective truth or to have universal meaning. This is a problem of language that begets a problem of identity. Since language is said to no longer express anything meaningful, we can no longer have stories, ideas, or theories that reliably explain to us who we are and in what to believe. There remain only conventions based on a certain consensus that govern common life, but whose value is purely contingent, unencumbered by any claim to express universal values or truths. There are not so much truths, postmodernism insists, as there are incommensurable local linguistic systems. Everything is understood in a global framework in which difference is not or should not be a cause of conflict, because all linguistic systems are equally valid in their context and can coexist peacefully, indifferent to each other.

Some think that the cause of this cultural context is capitalism or, more generally, the market economy and the powerful consumerist thrust on which it rests.[21] This consumerist push triggers an exponential development of advertising, which in turn stimulates the need for a product not for its actual utility, but for the symbolic value it represents in the consumer's imagination. For example, today we buy an iPhone not because we need it, but because it symbolizes the modern lifestyle.

The symbol is thus dissociated from reality, and this paradigm progressively extends not only to every form of language but also to the perception that contemporary humanity has of itself. Untethered from any normative identity, free to construct its own image on the basis of the symbols offered on the market, the self has an intoxicating freedom, but it is a freedom that, in the absence of limits and purpose, finds itself at the mercy of disillusionment and anxiety. The contemporary or "postmodern" self is vulnerable to this alternation between inebriation and disillusion, unable to

---

21. Cf. Kenneth D. Allan, "The Postmodern Self: A Theoretical Consideration," *Quarterly Journal of Ideology* 20 (1997): 3–24.

grasp a reliable meaning of one's own existence in the absence of a universally credible language.[22]

But beyond this cultural analysis, for a philosophical genealogy of postmodernism, we have to go back to the nihilism of Nietzsche and in particular to its identification of reason with power. According to Nietzsche, every discourse that claims to be coherent is actually an expression and instrument of arbitrary power; as a result, every discourse, every narrative today is suspect and must be constantly deconstructed in order to expose its arbitrariness; if a value or a belief prevails, it is only because it has succeeded in imposing itself through violence.

We don't need to undertake a critique of these positions here, but it was necessary to mention them in order to focus on one of the fundamental obstacles that any attempt to express a meaning faces in the contemporary world. This can be stated as follows: Does a language still exist that is able to express and convey meaning and identity today?

With regard to this devaluation of language and "relativism," we can be indignant, denounce them from philosophical and theological points of view, and can hope that they evolve in a way that we consider more favorable to the proclamation of faith. Or, on the basis of what we have considered thus far, we can seek a theological and spiritual response of a sapiential nature, based on solidarity, appreciation of historicity, and generous dialogue.

Solidarity is not condescension; it is founded on an authentic and humble self-understanding. Instead of looking at postmodern culture or any other phenomenon from above or from outside, it is first necessary to recognize its effects on oneself. We must therefore ask ourselves: How much are we, each of us, voluntarily or involuntarily, consciously or unconsciously, "postmodern"? How much does the suspicion of any normative discourse or belief characterize each of us, even believers, by the very fact that we are

---

22. Cf. Kenneth D. Allan, "A Formalization of Postmodern Theory," *Sociological Perspectives* 43 (2000) 3: 363–385.

part of this world, this time, this culture? Are we also dedicated to this constant deconstruction of every discourse, narrative, and even our own creed? Or again, how much of the heterogeneous, multi-form, eclectic character of postmodernism characterizes each of us? Are we not all inclined to make our own synthesis, to more or less pick and choose what we like, both in innocuous areas such as clothing, for example, but also in ethics and faith, the values and rules that establish common life?

The point of acknowledging these things about ourselves here is not to assign blame, but simply to note a fact. Paradoxically, one of the most glaring examples of the postmodern mentality in the recent history of the church has been the establishment of two "forms" of a single liturgical rite, one called "ordinary" and the other called "extraordinary," despite the fact that they rest on two different anthropologies and on two sometimes contradictory theological approaches to redemption and the church. This is an example of the typical postmodern attitude highlighted above: different cultures, antagonistic to each other, can coexist with relative indifference because their value depends only on their internal consistency.

Taking history seriously and being magnanimous in dialogue (the second and third sapiential attitudes) in our approach to postmodernism therefore means carefully considering what language we must use in order to communicate effectively within today's culture and mentality; to actually "go into the whole world" as Jesus commands—that is, to bring the gospel to where people really are today and not where we would like them to be; to address all cultures, all categories of people, and not just the ones we are comfortable with.

Here we mention the work of theorists like John Milbank[23] or George Lindbeck,[24] whose attempts to propose a theology

---

23. Cf. John Milbank, *Theology and Social Theory: Beyond Secular Reason* (Cambridge, MA: Blackwell, 1991); Milbank, "Postmodern Critical Augustinianism," in John Milbank and Oliver Simon, eds., *The Radical Orthodoxy Reader* (London: Routledge, 2009), 225–237.

24. Cf. George A. Lindbeck, *The Nature of Doctrine: Religion and Theology in a Postliberal Age* (Philadelphia: Westminster Press, 1984).

in a postmodern framework had a large impact in the Anglo-American sphere. There's no need to offer a critical evaluation of their thinking here, but simply to draw inspiration from some of their proposals to better appreciate what a theological response with a sapiential approach might look like.

John Milbank, in his book *Theology and Social Theory*, seeks a language for faith in a postmodern framework. His proposal can be summarized as follows: Since postmodernism no longer believes in discourses and narratives, but is based only on culture and social interactions, it is on this ground that it must be engaged. This means that the church should not preoccupy itself primarily with the construction of a discourse (or, even worse, an apologetics), but with the creation of a context, a culture, a space, a process—that is, a community where coexistence is based not on arbitrariness and violence, as nihilism suggests, but on peace and the integration of difference.

In other words, the language we need to use is the eloquence of the Christian community itself; the witness of community life "speaks" by itself. The Christian God can be thought of and proposed only as a God who is worshiped and imagined, who inspires a certain way of living and a certain space in which people can find and offer hospitality. The language that *is* the Christian community cannot be justified as more rational or, outside of its discourse, more desirable than nihilism or all the other alternatives present in the contemporary cultural arena; the language that *is* the Christian community can simply be proposed as an alternative or, if nothing else, claim a position that is neither more nor less legitimate than that of any other language. In this sense, postmodernism proves to be a somewhat more favorable context for Christianity than modernity, because at least postmodernism does not deny Christianity the right to exist.

Both Lindbeck's and Milbank's thinking are probably too minimalist from a theological point of view, and it is difficult not to have reservations about their conception of the relationship between the word of God and the church. But the proposal outlined above, with its accent on the eloquence of the Christian community itself, is compelling. The witness of community life is eloquent, speaks by itself, evangelizes not by relying on theoretical persuasion ("apologetics"), but by practicing hospitality, inclusion, listening, and the integration of difference in a context created by a common listening to the word of God. It is precisely here that we can perhaps better appreciate the contribution of monasticism to the sapiential way of doing theology.

Sapiential aspects of monastic life

So, (1) a full integration of one's humanity—that is, to be in contact with oneself, with history, with the world; (2) the ability to take an interest in the world as world, without fear of secularity; (3) reason that does not seek conclusions too rapidly or easily—these are the characteristics of the sapiential attitude.

Further, (1) solidarity as an awareness, not as condescension; (2) a full acceptance of the historical dimension of our identity, both personal and ecclesial; (3) a general openness to dialogue and integration of all that is human—these are the values that must characterize the presence and action of the church in the contemporary world, according to the Second Vatican Council.

Finally, a community life that speaks for itself in the way it offers a space for the integration of difference that is neither conflictual nor neutral, because it is characterized by a nonviolent but peaceful dialectic—this is the language or, if we wish, the manner of doing theology that still seems to guarantee a transmission of meaning in the current cultural context.

This simple list of key elements that have emerged so far has a strong affinity with the monastic vocation and demonstrates its potential. To make these aptitudes explicit and proceed in our reflection, it will be useful to ask ourselves what real solidarity with the "world" consists of. There have been many attempts to implement this solidarity in the decades that followed the Second Vatican Council, but the scarcity of tangible results and today's crisis of Christianity are inescapable indicators of their failure.

Already in the 1970s, there was, for example, an interest in the world as world without fear of secularity, but it was often translated into a mere secularization, that is, a dilution of the Christian identity. Instead of bringing the leaven of the Gospel to the heart of the world, many Christians succumbed to the seductions, idolatry, individualism, narcissism, and hedonism of the world. This clearly is not the sapiential attitude of the Bible nor the solidarity advocated by *Gaudium et Spes*. For this reason, it is not surprising to witness today the proliferation of the opposite tendency—the resurgence of clericalism, a hypervigilance about identity within the church, a cultural and political antagonism toward the world, a demonization of secularity, and a stigmatization of contemporary culture simplistically dismissed as "relativist."

The reason for this failure can be easily understood in light of an authentically sapiential attitude: the possibility of being interested in the world as world without fear of secularity becomes an instrument to help us grow in wisdom only if it is accompanied by a full understanding and integration of one's own humanity; we can enter into real contact with the world and with history only if we engage in the difficult and often painful ascesis of self-knowledge; we have the promise of gaining an understanding of the truth only if we genuinely preserve the form of charity—that is, a real sense of responsibility toward our own community of belonging.

This is the fundamental lesson of monasticism: monastics do not flee the world, but take a certain distance from the world to enter into a more profound relationship with it; they do not choose community life in order to withdraw in an ideal environment of coexistence, sheltered from the difficulties of the contemporary world; they choose it because community life lived responsibly is the most effective way of testing the authenticity of self-knowledge, of one's own conversion, of one's relationship with God.

The key to everything, then, is in this relationship with God and in the means, values, and criteria that guarantee its genuineness in the monastic tradition. These means, values, and criteria can be summarized as follows. First, the primacy attributed not to the work of humanity for God, but to the *opus Dei*, the work of God on our behalf, offered to us through ongoing exposure to God's word in liturgical celebration and personal meditation. Second, the relationship with time rooted in the rhythms of daily prayer and work that, even if it does not eliminate all worries, at least relativizes them, supporting one's availability to God, *vacare Deo*. Third, the eschatological orientation of monastic life symbolically (and bodily) represented, for example, by the *vigil*: in it, by taking time from one's sleep, the monk takes nothing away from his own ethical duty toward the world, but claims a space in which every worldly logic can, at least provisionally, be placed in brackets to give first place to the relationship with God.[25] Fourth, the full integration of bodiliness in one's relationship with God, which leads to being just as attentive to prayer as to work, to *lectio divina* as to eating and sleeping. And fifth, a common life marked by peace, by the full acceptance of difference and patience.

Peace

It is not by chance that the very word *peace, pax*, has become the motto that best sums up the monastic charism. To conclude our reflections, let's consider this peace and the acceptance of difference and patience that it entails.

The nihilistic dialectic we mentioned above presupposes that human relationships are marked by arbitrary power and violence. Differences are irreconcilable, equivocal, and only those who succeed in imposing themselves on others survive. According to the celebrated scapegoat dynamics explored by René Girard, violence is periodically transferred to a victim designated on the basis of its difference from the rest of the group.[26] But the space opened by the relationship with God—or rather, by the covenant that God establishes with humanity—replaces this violent paradigm

25. Cf. Lacoste, *Expérience et absolu*.
26. René Girard, *The Scapegoat*, trans. Yvonne Freccero (Baltimore: Johns Hopkins University Press, 1989).

with one of peace that, although not yet fully realized, even if it is eschatological, actually already inaugurates a new model of common life in the church and in the monastic community. In the space inhabited by the Christian community, the rich and the poor, the noble and the commoner, people of different races and even of enemy nations become one community that prays and works together. This means that the violence of history, although not eliminated, is, in this communal space, at least relativized.

The novelty of this "pre-eschatological" peace is manifest particularly in a management of *difference* that overcomes both the violence of nihilism and the indifference of postmodernism. Indeed, with nihilism, difference is equivocal and always generates violent opposition. Postmodernism opts for indifference so that even opposing beliefs can coexist with each other, confined as they are in autonomous spaces or systems that do not interact or interact only superficially. We know well that Christianity is not immune to either of these dynamics—the Creed becomes an occasion for division, violence, compulsion, or, in reaction, we often have promoted models of tolerance that prefer to ignore differences as if they did not exist or were irrelevant.

Instead, an authentic Christian community promotes, protects, and guarantees the freedom to be different and at the same time rejects indifference. Summarizing the thought of the British theologian Rowan Williams, Benjamin Myers proposes observations that are quite relevant in this regard:

> Social life is not about collapsing differences or artificial unity. Instead differences should be accentuated as sharply as possible, so that what you experience in another person is not fantasy, not another deceptive projection of yourself, but the real intractable mystery of another self . . . . [Rowan] Williams has groped towards a third way, in which difference is neither absolutized nor abolished, but tenuously preserved; my own identity emerges from the hard work of sustaining the difference between myself and others.[27]

27. Myers, *Christ the Stranger*, 17, 51.

Moreover, the language represented by the common life is manifest in the form of *patience*, which is also very present in Williams's thought:

> This means the church will be a community marked by patience. It will look for its own identity as something not yet possessed. Here the church is sustained by what Sergius Bulgakov has called "the patience of the Spirit." In the Holy Spirit, God is patient with us just as a parent is lovingly patient with the slow growth of a child. Indeed the Spirit is God's patience, God's own commitment to the slow process of growth and transformation, and to those fringe dwellers who remain remote from the church's visible centre. For Williams, the same is often true of the Christian life: if we're not growing daily, almost imperceptibly, then we're not growing at all. Patience means endurance of hardship, a willingness to tarry with the experience of failure and incompleteness. But God does not stand aloof from our tragic experience; in the Holy Spirit, God bears our struggle and sustains it. [28]

The same message resounds in a striking 2005 homily given by Pope Benedict XVI on the day of the inauguration of his Petrine ministry:

> It is not power, but love that redeems us! This is God's sign: he himself is love. How often we wish that God would show himself stronger, that he would strike decisively, defeating evil and creating a better world. All ideologies of power justify themselves in exactly this way, they justify the destruction of whatever would stand in the way of progress and the liberation of humanity. We suffer on account of God's patience. And yet, we need his patience. God, who became a lamb, tells us that the world is saved by the Crucified One, not by those

28. Myers, *Christ the Stranger*, 57.

who crucified him. The world is redeemed by the patience of God. It is destroyed by the impatience of man.[29]

All of this demands that theology escapes the too-tight (and artificial) circle of *fides et ratio*, the simple dialectic between faith and reason, and recovers anew the wings provided by the Augustinian perspective of reason based on love. In fact, the phrase (one could almost say the slogan) *fides et ratio* is often taken to mean a truth that one would like to consider as secure and certain for everyone, always and in every place, and above all that would not need to be loved in order to be known. But a truth that is at our complete disposal in this way risks becoming an idol.[30] If we instead accept that love and faith cannot be separated[31] because God is love, then knowledge of God (and of truth) will result from an act that involves rationality, experience, and freedom—that is, that integrates our entire humanity, embraces history, and accepts the need to manage difference.[32]

Truth that does not take the form of charity is not the truth of Christ. A paradoxical manifestation of this shrinking of both reason and faith is the reversal of the New Testament's phrase *veritas in caritate*, "the truth in charity" (Eph 4:15) to *caritas in veritate*, "charity in truth."[33] Certainly, it all depends on how we

29. Pope Benedict XVI, "Homily for the Beginning of the Petrine Ministry of the Bishop of Rome" (April 24, 2005): https://w2.vatican.va/content/benedict-xvi /en/homilies/2005/documents/hf_ben-xvi_hom_20050424_inizio-pontificato.html.

30. Lacoste, *The Appearing of God*, 70–71: "'Natural knowledge' and 'pure reason' place us firmly in the realm of what pretends to be *certain*, certain for all, certain always and everywhere, known without anyone having to *want* to know. Nature and natural knowledge are fascinating, since their truth lies open to us."

31. Lacoste, 74: "The co-originary status of faith and love makes it impossible to have a theology of faith that is not also a theory of the love of God."

32. Lacoste, 104: "When 'created' realities (which at first we do not know to be created) draw our attention to a 'Creator,' it is up to us in the totality of our mental powers—rationality, affection, decision—to accept the indication they provide."

33. Cf. the title of Pope Benedict's 2009 encyclical letter *Caritas in Veritate*.

mean this latter expression, and it would be naive to deny the constant risk of turning charity into empty sentimentality when it is untethered from the objective content of faith. But from the epistemological point of view, St. Paul's ordering of the relationship between truth and charity must not be inverted, because it is the only way that allows us to take seriously both charity and history. Inverting *veritas in caritate* as *caritas in veritate* can lead to restricting charity to our limited (because it is pre-eschatological) perception of truth.

And if we think about it, this is what faith in YHWH is about. The Lord refuses to give his name. "I am who I am" (Exod 3:14) means "I am the one who acts as he acts," "I am the one whose identity is manifested in his acting." And indeed, the Lord first establishes the relationship, the covenant, enters our history, starts with us from where we are, then leads us into the desert to speak to our heart (Hos 2:16) and only within the dynamic of this *hesed*, this love, this patience, bearing the weight of our slowness and our resistance, introduces us, by means of the Spirit, "to all truth" (John 16:13). The name of God, YHWH, implies that taking history and our humanity seriously is not simply the expression of God's condescension, but belongs to his identity. All the more reason it must belong to the identity of God's people, God's children, God's church.

In conclusion, then, a sapiential theology inspired by monasticism reestablishes the vital link between theology and the church understood as a community created by God's word and God's love and sustained by God's patience. This community lives in the covenant with God and is made up of a people that journeys through the history of this world with the mission of embracing the whole of humanity. Just as God takes this process seriously and patiently waits for history to unfold, so God also invites Christians to a profound acceptance of their humanity, to commit themselves fully to history, not to fear secularism, and to dedicate themselves fully to solidarity, hospitality, and dialogue.

CONCLUSION

A Spirituality for the Church

A life built on the recitation of the psalms is one in which it is possible to understand all daily human experience as capable of being taken up and transformed by God in Jesus.

Rowan Williams[1]

There is something of a fixation in the West with the specific identities of the numerous religious orders that have flourished since the end of the Middle Ages. When we speak of a religious order's *charism*, we refer to aspects of mission or spirituality that distinguish one order from all the others. This rhetoric of specialization was not nearly as prominent among the first great historical religious orders (Carthusians, Dominicans, Franciscans) but grew over time with the introduction of distinctions that were unknown during the first millennium, such as that between contemplative life and active life, between monks and brothers or nuns and sisters. Religious orders have exponentially increased their focus on very specific aspects of the church's mission (for example, the redemption of slaves or the pastoral care of migrants), on forms

---

1. Williams, *The Way of St Benedict*, 47.

of piety that reflect the spirituality of the epochs in which the orders were born (prayer for the souls in purgatory, perpetual Eucharistic adoration, or devotion to the Sacred Heart), on certain institutional forms (absolute or relative centralization), or even on liturgical rites (for example, the so-called "extraordinary form" of the Roman rite).

Without wishing to critically evaluate this logic, but taking it as a matter of fact, we can note that in some religious orders it has sometimes caused a weakening of the sense of ecclesial communion, untethered them from the liturgical life of the broader church, or fostered an isolation and separation that, as time went by, resulted in ecclesial barrenness—that is, the inability to remain open to the breath of the Spirit to recognize the signs of the times—and a consequent vocational crisis.

Embracing everything and everyone

From a theological point of view, the fruitfulness of any religious order and indeed of any Christian community depends on two factors. First, the extent to which they promote ecclesial communion in the local church, that is the place where we actually are in contact with the neighbor we are called to love. Second, the extent to which they make the mystery of the church visible. In the Creed, we confess that the church is one, holy, catholic, and apostolic. Catholicity here is particularly important. Every community becomes an authentic sign of the church only if it is *catholic*—that is open to the whole, embracing everything and everyone.

These factors have underpinned our endeavors to capture some of the key aspects of the spirituality of Benedictine monasticism throughout this book. Tackling this issue by looking for the specificity of the Benedictine order, for what makes it unlike any other religious order in the West, would lead down a wrong path. To give just one example, people sometimes ask whether Benedictine monasticism is active or contemplative, without realizing that these categories are anachronistic: Benedictines appeared several centuries before the distinction between contemplative life and active life was devised with the purpose of differentiating orders dedicated exclusively to prayer from orders that pursed pastoral activities. Instead, we have tried to simply find out how Benedictine spirituality is *catholic*—that is encompassing the whole breadth of God's plan of salvation for the world. In this concluding chapter we shall sum up this line of inquiry from the viewpoint of an aspect of Benedictine monasticism we have encountered at almost every step—namely the priority given to the *opus Dei*, the "Work of God," which is far more than the simple celebration of the liturgy.

Beyond the great differences in the ways the Rule is lived in various monastic families, the organization of the day around the celebration of the Liturgy of the Hours remains their most visible common activity. Furthermore, it is an aspect that can be easily recognized even by those who know nothing about Benedictine life. In keeping with the ideas noted above, let us consider how the *opus Dei* makes Benedictine spirituality an ecclesial spirituality, exploring its meaning from the two complementary viewpoints that we have met several times already: "theological" in the sense of *what one believes*, that is creeds and doctrines; and "spiritual" in the sense of *how one believes*, that is the way in which our trust in God becomes a living and loving relationship with the God of Jesus Christ and shapes our lives in a defining way.

The real work

Benedict's Rule ascribes the same primacy to both the love of Christ and the *opus Dei*. The importance of both is expressed by the adverb *nihil*, "nothing": "Nothing must come before the love of Christ" (RB 4.21)[2] and "Nothing is to be preferred to the work of God" (RB 43.3). This parallel, even if it is not intentional—indeed,

---

2. *Nihil amori Christi praeponere* (in RB80: "the love of Christ must come before all else"). Cf. RB 72.11, *Christo omnino nihil praeponant* ("Prefer nothing whatever to Christ") and RB 5.2, *Haec convenit his qui nihil sibi a Christo carius aliquid existimant* (". . . which comes naturally to those who cherish Christ above all").

especially if it is not intentional—expresses something profound about the meaning of the expression *opus Dei*: the work of God and the love of Christ are the same reality, and this explains why they are credited with the same prominence.

The love of Christ here means first of all *Christ's love for us*; it is only secondly our love for Christ. In turn, this prompts a question about the expression *opus Dei*: Why call the communal celebration of the Liturgy of the Hours "*opus Dei*," a work not of humanity but of God? From a theological point of view, the answer is simple: Because the liturgy is acceptance and celebration of what God alone does, God alone gives, and to which we can respond only by means of a gift from God.

The Gospel of John speaks of both the *works* of God (in the plural) and the *work* of God (in the singular). We find it in the plural several times when Jesus says, "Whoever believes in me will do the works that I do, and will do greater ones than these, because I am going to the Father" (John 14:10-12)—here it designates actions we are supposed to accomplish ourselves. But we find it in the singular in the following passage: "So they said to him, 'What can we do to accomplish the works of God?' Jesus answered and said to them, 'This is the work of God, that you believe in the one he sent'" (John 6:28-29). To the disciples who ask him what the works of God are—that is, the works that people should do *for God*—Jesus responds by turning their perspective upside down: before speaking of the works of humanity for God, it is necessary to welcome the work of God *for humanity*, the *opus Dei*, what God works in us—that is, the gift of faith. Now, in the Gospel of John and in the New Testament faith does not designate primarily the content to be believed, but the gift of a relationship with God, the gift of fellowship with God—faith is not first of all "the doctrines I have to believe" but "a trust in God that shapes my life in a characteristic way" by generating fellowship—as we read in the 1 John, where it is said that the reason for announcing the Gospel is that those who receive it "may have fellowship with us" (cf. 1 John 1:1-4).

Therefore, the *opus Dei* is what God works in us. The Rule's "*nihil operi Dei praeponatur*" doesn't mean "put nothing before the works that *we* must do for God," but rather "put nothing before welcoming and celebrating what *God* does for us, that is God's work of salvation in us—the covenant, reconciliation, communion with God."

This is a radically transformed understanding of the *opus Dei*. It reestablishes the primacy of the Lord's initiative and action. The accent is no longer on how we celebrate the Liturgy of the Hours but on what *the Lord does* through liturgy. In this perspective, "to put nothing before welcoming and celebrating what God does for us" means that we are continually called together into the covenant by the word of God; that is, we are invited to be ever more deeply *reconciled* with the Father and with our sisters and brothers. Then it means responding to this grace with the thanksgiving that is the Eucharistic celebration and its prolongation, the psalmody, whose nature is essentially communal. In the liturgy, we celebrate the gift of God that is grace by giving thanks, by offering gift in exchange for gift, and in this way we become, in union with Christ, a sacrifice pleasing to God. This covenant and this reconciliation become manifest in loving lived fellowship because this is the sign of a grace that is communion—in other words, if the gift that we receive is fellowship and we welcome it with an open and sincere heart, then it cannot but become visible in the quality and fruitfulness of our community life.

All together

Saint Benedict had a clear awareness of all of this. Indeed, in his Rule both the sentences that we have taken as a starting point— "Nothing is to be preferred to the work of God" (RB 43.3) and "Nothing must come before the love of Christ" (RB 4.21; cf. RB 72.11 and 5.2)—are quoted in chapters that place the essentially communal character of salvation at the center of the monastics' life.

Thus, in connection to the priority of the work of God, the Rule states that the whole community should participate to the celebration of the office (the *Opus Dei*) and for its entire duration. Only the abbot can dispense the monastic from participating in it. Even when monastics are away from the monastery, they must recite the office at the set times, wherever they are (RB 50). What matters in these norms is not the "letter" but the "spirit"—that is, the spiritual insight they entail: the fellowship generated by God's gift is most visible during the communal celebration of the liturgy.

We find this same basic vision expressed elsewhere in the Rule—for example, in the chapters dedicated to the excommunication of monks who have committed faults (RB 23–30; 43–44). Today the word *excommunication* has lost the depth of its original, ecclesial meaning. In the Rule of Benedict, it is an "exclusion from visible communion" with a medicinal purpose—that is, a means of healing, a way to help monastics to understand the true extent of the faults that damage community life and introduce divisions, especially pride, gossip, and disobedience (RB 23.1). Excommunication is meant to help recalcitrant monastics to become aware of the seriousness of the consequences of their behavior on the community. This explains why, for Benedict, the fundamental prerequisite for administering the penalty of excommunication is the ability of the one receiving it to understand its gravity: "let the monk be excommunicated, provided that he understands the nature of this punishment" (RB 23.4); unusually for his time, even young monks or boys should be punished in this way only if they can "understand the seriousness of the penalty of excommunication" (RB 30.2). Physical isolation helps monastics to understand how much more serious is the moral isolation in which they close themselves up by separating themselves from their brothers and sisters with disdainful attitudes. Now, in the Rule, the most serious form of excommunication concerns precisely the celebration of the liturgy. It can range from the prohibition of playing an active role in prayer (intoning psalms, proclaiming readings) (RB 24.2; 44.4-6) to simple exclusion from the oratory (RB 25.1; 44). Again, what matters here is the spiritual insight presupposed by these norms; namely that our prayer is pleasing to God only if it is done in union with Christ and with his body the church. The monastics who have damaged community life with their behavior must understand the consequences of their actions through exclusion from the common celebration of the liturgy.

The second expression, "Nothing must come before the love of Christ," is also set in a communal context—indeed, it is part of the well-known chapter 72 of the Rule, which is widely recognized as one of the most inspiring pages of the Benedictine code:

> Just as there is a wicked zeal of bitterness which separates from God and leads to hell, so there is a good zeal which separates from evil and leads to God and everlasting life. This, then, is the good zeal which monks must foster with fervent love: 'They should each try to be the first to show respect to the other' (Rom 12:10), supporting with the greatest patience one another's weaknesses of body or behavior, and earnestly competing in obedience to one another. No one is to pursue what he judges better for himself, but instead, what he judges better for someone else. To their fellow monks they show the pure love of brothers; to God, loving fear; to their abbot, unfeigned and humble love. Let them prefer nothing whatever to Christ, and may he bring us all together to everlasting life.

The way of fulfilling the injunction "Nothing must come before the love of Christ" is by caring for each other in community life. We are truly celebrating the *opus Dei*, that is welcoming God's reconciliation and prioritizing the love of Christ above everything else, only when we respect one another, bear one another's faults with patience, are open to one another, look out not for our own interests but those of others. And the communal nature of salvation culminates in the "all together" that concludes this chapter: "and may Christ bring us all together to everlasting life." Benedictine monastics do not seek to flourish individually or in competition with each other, but jointly, cooperatively.

Therefore, when we ask about the spirituality of Benedictine monasticism, it is in this priority (*nihil preponatur, nihil praeponere, pariter*) that we will find it: Nothing may be put before the Father's work of salvation in us through Christ in the Holy Spirit, which is covenant, reconciliation, communion. Nothing is more important than the celebration of this love in prayer and in a fraternal life that makes this grace visible. Nothing can be put before fellowship—that is, this community of which I am a part and the local church in which it is inserted. In the upbuilding of this fellowship I must pour all my heart, soul, and strength. Finally, nothing can be put before this *pariter:* there is no real joy if we do not reach the finish line together.

Communion as mission

Therefore, this dual prioritization of the *work of God* and the *love of Christ* offers a sound response to the question we have sought to answer in this book: defining what is specific to Benedictine spirituality from the point of view of what makes it authentically catholic, an "expression of the whole," so as to be "prophecy for the whole."

This leads us to the final step in our search: pointing out the main contribution of Benedictine monasticism to the spiritual life of the church.

The logic of specialization in religious life in the church in the West, in addition to the disadvantages that we mentioned above, has another drawback. Religious orders born after the Middle Ages have tended to express their specific characteristics, their charism, not in terms of *communion* but of *mission*. That is, they identified themselves on the basis of aspects of the mission of the church particularly urgent in the era in which they were founded—preaching, care for the sick, teaching, pastoral care of young people, evangelization through mass media, and so on. In the new forms of religious life, the structure of community life was nearly always ancillary to its apostolic needs, communion was subordinated to mission.

Benedictine monasticism, on the other hand, despite having carried out almost all these same activities and many others, has

never defined itself by identifying with any of them. Throughout
the winding path of its history, including some missteps, it has
continued to recognize itself always and first of all in the double
nihil praeponatur for the work of God and the love of Christ, and
in the *pariter*, the priority given to communion over mission, in
the belief that *the most powerful form of mission was precisely communion itself.*

The priority given to communion in the Rule of Benedict is
not a form of collective egoism, comparable to the ethnic or social
particularism that leads regions, races, nations, or social classes to
close in on themselves. On the contrary, it is a preference for a
love that does not close in on itself, but reaches out and is prophetic; indeed that is prophecy par excellence because it speaks
not so much through words but through life. When it is lived as
it should be, Benedictine spirituality transforms communities
into lamps set on a lampstand. This is what Jesus says when he
declares, "This is how all will know that you are my disciples, if
you have love for one another" (John 13:35). Or again, it is what
the theologian Hans Urs von Balthasar implies in the title of one
of his most well-known works: love alone is credible.[3]

The history of Benedictine monasticism is eloquent in this
regard: every time this priority has faded into the background and
an attempt has been made to subordinate the framework of community life to a very noble missionary purpose, the beginnings may
sometimes have been exhilarating, but a crisis has almost always
ensued. It is not that such efforts are illegitimate; indeed, over the
course of the 1,500 years of their history, Benedictine monastics
have carried out almost all the activities that have been adopted
as the particular identities of more recently created religious orders, and the decisive contribution of Benedictine monasteries
to the history of European civilization and culture is universally

---

3. Hans Urs von Balthasar, *Love Alone Is Credible*, trans. D. C. Schindler (San
Francisco: Ignatius Press, 2004); orig. ed. *Glaubhaft ist nur liebe* (Einsiedeln:
Johannes Verlag, 1968).

recognized. This apostolic, cultural, and social fruitfulness is an expression of the flexibility and genius of Benedictine monasticism.

At the same time, however, Benedictine communities have never defined themselves based on the activities they have carried out at a given moment in their history. If this had happened, these same communities would have lost their raison d'être when the need for such activities had ceased. This has happened to some modern religious orders that have linked their identity too narrowly to certain aspects of the church's mission. This is, for example, the case of some religious orders created to provide health care or education that are now extinct because these services were taken up by civil society.

Several Benedictine monasteries run schools, universities, hospitals, or work in mission territories, but they always try to safeguard the priority of communion over mission, or rather the priority of communion as the most important form of the mission. Thus monastics devote themselves to their many activities only to the extent that these activities do not interfere with the primacy (*nihil praeponatur*) reserved for the *opus Dei*, not only in the liturgical sense but precisely in the sense we mention above—that is, the primacy of welcoming and celebrating reconciliation, covenant, and fellowship through prayer and community life.

Such freedom is the highest expression of charity and generates a characteristic joy: *Ecce quam bonum et quam iucundum habitare fratres in unum*, "How good and how pleasant it is, when brothers dwell together as one!" (Ps 133:1). It is the joy that comes from communion lived by reconciled people of which John speaks in the passage of his first letter quoted above: "We are writing this so that our joy may be complete" (1 John 1:4).

In conclusion, therefore, the defining contribution of Benedictine monasticism to the church and the world is its *ecclesial* and *catholic* spirituality: thanks to the double prioritization of the work of God and of the love of Christ, its *nihil praeponatur* and its *pariter*, the Benedictine monastery is meant to be a sign and a prophecy of what the church is.

Indeed, Jesus assigns this double priority to the whole church: before it can be an instrument of salvation or, better still, in order to be an instrument of salvation, the church must be, first of all and in an ever more transparent way, a sign of salvation. And since salvation is reconciliation and fellowship, it is proclaimed in a credible way only when it becomes flesh in a community marked and guided by charity, joy, and the freedom of the children of God. In this way, communion becomes the most important means of evangelization, because loving fellowship alone is worthy of faith. Love alone is credible.